Bold
Robert Emmet

1778-1803

Bold Robert Emmet

1778-1803

Seán Ó Brádaigh

Nár lean Wolfe Tone an ród seo i ngéibheann
Ar shráideanna naofa Áth' Cliath,
Is an Gearaltach óg gan fóir dá chéasadh
Ar shráideanna naofa Áth' Cliath,
Agus Emmet sa charr ar lá sin an sceoin
Is a leicne bána gan scáth ná deoir
Ag feitheamh le bás is miongháire ar a bheol,
Ar shráideanna naofa Áth' Cliath?

An tAthair Pádraig de Brún,
Samhain, 1923

Cló Saoirse – Irish Freedom Press

First published in Ireland, April 2003, by
Cló Saoirse – Irish Freedom Press
223 Parnell Street, Dublin 1.

ISBN 0 9518567 7 4

Cover designed by Níall Funge
*Based on 'The Execution of Robert Emmet, in Thomas Street,
20th September 1803'. Courtesy of the National Library of Ireland*
Typeset in Adobe Garamond
Book designed and printed by
Elo Press Ltd., Dublin 8

BUÍOCHAS

My aim in writing and compiling this book, with its appendices, was to prepare a short account of the life of Robert Emmet for the general reader. In doing this, I consulted most of the literature which has been produced on this subject, over the last two hundred years, by many researchers and historians, beginning with Dr Richard R Madden. I am grateful to all of them. Their names are listed in the Bibliography.

The scholarly work of Leon Ó Broin and Patrick M Geoghegan was particularly valuable and useful to me. I would recommend their published works to any reader of this book who wishes to obtain a more comprehensive account of the story of Robert Emmet.

I should like also to thank Leita Ní Chathmhaoil and Róisín Hayden for their generous assistance and Elo Press for their high standard of presentation.

Seán Ó Brádaigh

CHAPTER ONE

—◆—

Bold Robert Emmet, the darling of Erin,
Bold Robert Emmet will die with a smile,
Farewell companions both loyal and daring
I'll lay down my life for the Emerald Isle.

ROBERT EMMET is remembered mostly as a young Dublin man who planned and led an unsuccessful insurrection against English rule in 1803, who made an eloquent speech from the dock and who was hanged outside St. Catherine's Church in Dublin's Thomas Street.

A study of his life and work shows that he was a talented son of a respectable family, who displayed idealistic sincerity in his love of country and who faced his death at the age of 25 with fortitude and courage.

It is entirely appropriate that in the bicentenary year of his death for Ireland we should tell the story of this remarkable man.

Robert Emmet, the Irish patriot, was the seventeenth child born to Dr Robert Emmet and his wife Elizabeth Mason, who had married in 1760. Of these seventeen children only four survived. This gives us some idea of the awful infant mortality rate of the time. The father was a medical doctor and there is no evidence that the mother was delicate, so what must have been the hardship of the masses of ordinary people at that time?

These facts are worth mentioning for another reason also. Robert was in fact the fifth Robert to be born, as four other boys named Robert were born before him and died in infancy.

Dr Robert Emmet was born in Tipperary in 1729 and practised in Cork before coming to Dublin in 1770. The family lived first of all in Molesworth Street and later on St. Stephen's Green in a house which was separated from the College of Surgeons by Glover's Alley. The Doctor and his family were Protestants and were very well connected. He was appointed State Physician to the Viceregal household.

There was another deeper dimension to Dr. Emmet however. He was a

Robert Emmet

social reformer who was concerned particularly at the condition of Catholics under both English rule and the Irish Protestant Ascendancy. This idealistic Protestant gentleman broke with his family tradition and espoused the cause of Irish freedom. Like Theobald Wolfe Tone, he believed that separation from England was necessary in order to achieve the emancipation of the Irish people. He declared these views publicly in pamphlets which he wrote and eventually lost his state appointments. Idealism cost the Emmet family dearly.

Young Robert was born in the St. Stephen's Green house on March 4, 1778 and was baptised on March 10 in St Peter's Church of Ireland, Aungier Street. This church was demolished during the twentieth century. Some years later, the family moved to a detached house called 'Casino', in Milltown, near Bird Avenue.

Robert's eldest brother, Christopher Temple Emmet, was born in 1761 and had a short but brilliant career as a lawyer before his death at the age of 27. His only sister, Mary Anne Emmet, born in 1773, married a man called Robert Holmes. She was a classical scholar who wrote pamphlets for the United Irishmen. She died in 1804. Her husband was imprisoned for one year for his Republican activities, but he lived long enough to defend John Mitchel on a charge of treason-felony, in 1848.

In a brilliant address to the court, Holmes made references to the events of 1803, and declared:

> "Deep, deep, deep is the guilt of those who have made Irishmen slaves, and slaves' assassins, instead of leaving brave men free. Deep, deep, deep is the guilt of England, which, by an unprovoked and unjust invasion obtained dominion in Ireland."

Thomas Addis Emmet, born in 1764, was Robert's most famous sibling. He followed his father's footsteps and studied medicine, but changed later to law. One of his most famous cases was the defence of James Napper Tandy, a member of the United Irishmen, who was prosecuted on a charge of treason. Thomas Addis shocked the Establishment when he declared in the court: "there has been no legal viceroy in Ireland for the last six hundred years."

Thomas Addis himself was a member of the United Irishmen and was one of the members of the Leinster Directory arrested on March 12, 1798, before the Rising. He was held in Fort George in Scotland until his release

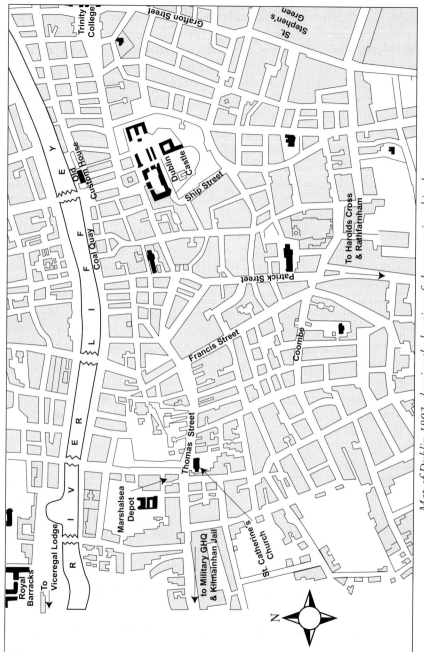

Map of Dublin 1803, showing the location of places mentioned in the text

Royal Barracks

To Viceregal Lodge

Marshalsea Depot

to Military GHQ & Kilmainham Jail

St. Catherine's Church

Thomas Street

Francis Street

Coombe

Patrick Street

To Harolds Cross & Rathfarnham

Dublin Castle

Ship Street

Old Custom House

Coal Quay

Trinity College

Grafton Street

St. Stephen's Green

RIVER LIFFEY

N

in 1802 following the signing of the Peace of Amiens in March 1802, which temporarily ended the war between England and France. He then went to France where he tried to influence the French Government to send an armed force to Ireland to assist another insurrection. He lost confidence in Napoleon Bonaparte who was then First Consul of France and he went to New York in 1804. He had a successful legal career there and became State Attorney of the State of New York. He died in 1827.

From his home on St. Stephen's Green Robert Emmet attended Oswald's School in Dopping Court, off Golden Lane, where he showed an aptitude for mathematics and science. From there he went to Samuel Whyte's school in Grafton Street, quite near his home, and later the school of the Rev. Mr Lewis in Camden Street. He entered Trinity College, Dublin in October 1793, at the age of fifteen and a half.

Robert was a brilliant student. He excelled at maths, science and physics, and he won several prizes. But it was mostly for his oratorical skills in the Historical and Debating Societies that his contemporaries in TCD remembered him afterwards. Naturally enough, the rights of man and the rights of Ireland were subjects on which he spoke passionately. He also wrote some poetry, using the pen name "Trebor", which was his own name Robert spelt in reverse.

One of his friends at TCD was Thomas Moore (of Moore's Irish Melodies fame), a Catholic. They had both been at Whyte's school and Moore's interest was in literature, the classics and music. He took many traditional Irish airs, like those collected by Edward Bunting and wrote lyrics in English to put with them. Moore tells the story of his playing the air of "Let Erin Remember the Days of Old" on the piano and Emmet declaring; "Oh, that I were at the head of twenty thousand men marching to that air!"

Moore spent many years in England afterwards and was a great favourite in society salons. His songs are still popular and many of them inspire patriotic feelings in Irish hearts the world over. In later years he paid Robert Emmet this generous tribute:

> "Were I to remember, indeed, among all I have known, who appeared to me to combine in the greatest degree, pure moral worth with intellectual power, I should, among the highest of the few, place Robert Emmet".

We have no record of Robert having played any part in the 1798 Rising, but in his college days he attended United Irishmen meetings in Thomas Addis's home. Because of his expertise in drawing and design he was asked to make a seal for the official organiser. The seal of the whole organisation was designed in the North, but Robert Emmet's seal was used for some time in the South. It was said, moreover, that the English government got their hands on an impression of it and used it as a decoy.

There were four branches of the United Irishmen in TCD and Robert Emmet was secretary of one of them. The authorities became worried and an enquiry was set up. Lord Chancellor Fitzgibbon, Earl of Clare, who was also Vice-Chancellor of the University, presided over what was called a "visitation", that is a kind of inquisition, which was held in April, 1798.

The students were put under oath and questioned about their political leanings and activities. Nineteen of them were expelled. Robert Emmet anticipated expulsion, ignored the proceedings and asked that his name be taken off the college rolls. We would say nowadays that he anticipated dismissal by offering his resignation.

On the second day of the inquiry, Emmet was not present. His tutor, Richard Graves, said that he had asked to have his name taken off the rolls.

Fitzgibbon accused Emmet in the following words:

> "I have been for some time in possession of everything that has been going forward in the college – and I know that Emmet is one of the most active and wicked members of the society of the United Irishmen – and I did desire the Provost not to suffer any person to take his name off the college books, that I might bring him and others of his association to punishment."

That Robert Emmet was a brilliant student there is no doubt. One of his childhood friends, who entered Trinity on the same day, was Archibald Douglas who became a renowned Protestant clergyman. He did not share Emmet's political views, but remembering him later, in 1842, he said:

> "So gifted a creature does not appear in a thousand years."

By the spring of 1798, Emmet was all set to graduate as a Bachelor of Arts. But his brother was arrested in March, and though he had asked to have his name taken off the rolls, to avoid Lord Clare's inquiry, his name was included

Thomas Addis Emmet

on the list of nineteen students who were expelled. George Keogh, son of the Catholic leader John Keogh, was also on that list, as was a man named Corbet who later became a general in the French army and another, Allen who became a colonel in the French army.

Robert Emmet's academic career was at an end. The doors of the professions in Dublin were now closed to him, because of the circumstances in which his studies at Trinity had come to an end. He considered trying to learn a trade and at some point thought of entering the leather business. One thing he did do was to become a committed revolutionary.

CHAPTER TWO

⫷◆⫸

IT WAS PROBABLY sometime during 1798 that Robert Emmet met Sarah Curran, with whom he was, and ever will be, romantically linked. She was the daughter of the eminent lawyer, John Philpot Curran.

A biographer of Curran relates:

> "Mr Robert Emmet, a young gentleman of highly respectable family, of very striking talents and interesting manners, was in the habit of visiting at Mr Curran's house."

When Theobald Wolfe Tone was under sentence of death in November 1798, having been tried by courtmartial, it was Curran who successfully obtained a writ of *habeas corpus* from the Chief Justice. Curran was attached to Henry Grattan's party, championed Catholic Emancipation and acted as a lawyer for some of the United Irishmen.

The Emmet and Curran families would have known each other. Richard Curran, Sarah's brother, was a Trinity student and may have introduced Robert to her. The lovers often met at the Curran country home, the "Priory" in Rathfarnham. The romance in the real sense seems to have begun sometime in the spring of 1803, and it appears to have been something of a secret affair. Her father discouraged her from seeing Robert because of his radical opinions. We know from correspondence that Robert shared his plans for the Rising with Sarah.

The whereabouts of Robert Emmet between about April 1799 and early 1801 are something of a mystery. We know that there was a warrant for his arrest in April 1799. *Habeas Corpus* had been suspended and he could be arrested and held for questioning, a kind of internment, until Major Charles Henry Sirr, the Head of the Dublin Police, known as the Town Provost, could get some informers to testify against him in open court. The suspension of *habeas corpus* lapsed on December 31, 1800 and the warrant would have lapsed with it. The Act of Union, which abolished the Irish parliament and created the United Kingdom of Great Britain and Ireland, came into force on the first day of the new century, January 1, 1801, and the restoration of *habeas corpus* was probably part of the English Government's new deal. By March 1801, however, it had been suspended again.

William Wickham, the Chief Secretary, wrote in a report dated December, 1803 (after Emmet's execution):

> "Early in the year 1801, Mr Robert Emmet went over to the Continent with a mission to the French Government from the Executive Directory of the United Irishmen here. He was accompanied by a Mr Malachi Delany of the County of Kildare; Delany had been formerly an officer in the Austrian service and was deeply engaged in the Rebellion of 1798. They travelled through England and embarked at Yarmouth for Hamburg, Emmet (against whom there was no charge) under his own name, and Delany under the name of Bowers... He returned to this country in November, 1802, where he remained unmolested, as he had done before, there being no charge against him, this circumstance of his having been sent on this treasonable mission having only been discovered since the Insurrection of the 23rd July."

Before travelling on to France Emmet visited his brother, Thomas Addis, in Fort George, He apparently visited Holland, Switzerland and Spain but made Paris his headquarters. There is a letter written by him from no 9 Rue D'Amboise, Paris, on October 6, 1801. In Paris he was busy lobbying for French assistance in the Irish cause. He had replaced Edward Lewins who had previously been the liaison officer between the Irish and French Republicans.

It was while he was in Paris that Emmet met an American engineering genius called Robert Fulton who passed on to him his ideas about building rockets, ideas which Emmet later developed further in Dublin.

He also studied manuals on military tactics. One book in particular he studied in great detail. This was a two-volume treatise by a colonel in the Prussian army called Georg Friederich von Tempelhoff. It was called *Extracts from Colonel Tempelhoff's History of the Seven Years War*, published in 1793. Emmet's copy is in the Royal Irish Academy in Dublin and the notes he made in the margins give an insight into his military thinking. For instance, the section on *patrols* is heavily annotated in pencil. He has underlined some sentences and drawn lines around paragraphs or sections of paragraphs to highlight them. The notes he has written in the margins are what we would now call sub-headings. Examples of what he wrote in this section are: "instructions to be given to patrols", "2 kinds of patrols", "precautions in case of ambuscade", "attention to byroads", "attention to villages", "woody heights", etc.

There was quite a large colony of Irish Republicans in Paris at this time. Following the signing of the Peace of Amiens by France and England in March, 1802, the Fort George prisoners were released and Thomas Addis Emmet, Thomas Russell, Arthur O'Connor, William McNeven and others made their way to Paris.

Russell, who was born in Kilshanick in north Co Cork in 1767, had served in the English army, was a United Man and a close friend of Tone, and was to have commanded Republican forces in Co Down in the 1798 Rising, but was arrested and jailed in 1796. He and Emmet appear to have been the prime movers in organising another insurrection.

Russell was a really outstanding man. While in Paris he and Emmet met General Jean-Joseph Humbert, who had landed in Co Mayo with a small French force in August 1798, rallied the pikemen of the West, won a spectacular victory over the English at Castlebar, proclaimed a Republic of Connacht and penetrated as far as Co Longford before being finally defeated. Humbert was anxious to come back again and join in another effort to liberate Ireland from English rule. Given his proven military ability and his experience in Ireland, his potential was considerable. Unfortunately, he was out of favour with Napoleon Bonaparte, who had seized power as First Consul of France in 1799.

In May, 1803 the war was renewed when Britain declared war on France. Thomas Addis recorded in his diary that he was informed that the French Government had decided, as part of the resumed hostilities, that an army of 25,000 men under General Massena would be sent to Ireland in about six months' time. November, 1803 was pencilled in as the target date for a rising at home. But Robert had already lost confidence in Bonaparte whom he had met, along with his Foreign Minister, the wily Charles Talleyrand. He did not like the means by which Bonaparte had seized power and felt that he was a tyrant in the making. He would, of course, have welcomed a French army, to support an Irish uprising, and there was talk of a rising in London, but in reality the Irish arena was not a priority for Bonaparte, and the army of 25,000 men never materialised.

Michael Dwyer

In fact, at this time an Irishman, born in Co Laois, then Queen's County, called Edward Marcus Despard, was planning a revolution in England. There was great unrest there, with food riots at the time. Despard's plan was to seize the king, government and higher officials and to rally the common people and set up a new democratic system of government. Despard was a friend of Lord Cloncurry, who was sympathetic to the United Irish cause and of a Mullingar man called William Dowdall who acted as an intermediary with Emmet. The authorities in London became aware of Despard's plans and he was arrested in November, 1802, tried and executed, along with six of his followers.

Robert Emmet returned to Ireland in October, 1802, and began to plan for a rising. He still kept a low profile and managed to avoid the police all along until his arrest on August 25, 1803. He probably spent some time at "Casino", which house was raided by Major Sirr in December, 1802. Robert was concealed in one of his hideouts on the premises. During this period he would have been in touch with Republicans from many parts of Ireland, survivors of 1798 who were still prepared to serve.

On March 7, 1803 at a meeting in Corbet's Hotel, 105 Capel Street, Dublin, Emmet briefed his key organisers. Shortly afterwards he leased premises at Marshalsea Lane/Mass Lane, off Thomas Street and set up an arms depot there.

During this time Major Sirr was anxious to track him down, but without success. He went as far as to ask Thomas Elrington, Senior Dean of TCD if he could provide a description of Emmet. This Elrington did and the following letter reveals how he helped to have one of the most distinguished students of TCD recognised by the police and eventually arrested, tried and hanged.

Letter from the Rev Thomas Elrington, DD, Senior Dean of Trinity College to Major Sirr.

7th June 1803.

Dear Sir, — Miss Bell having mentioned to me that you wished for a description of Robert Emmet, I send the best I can get of what he was five years ago. I know of no person who can give you an account of the alterations that may have taken place in his figure since.

Believe me, dear Sir,

Yours very truly,

Thomas Elrington.

He then added: "… In 1798 he was near twenty years of age, of an ugly sour countenance; small eyes, but not near-sighted; a dirty-brownish complexion; at a distance looks as if somewhat marked with small-pox; about five feet six inches high, rather thin than fat, but not of an emaciated figure; on the contrary, somewhat broad-made; walks briskly, but does not swing his arms."

This was a somewhat unflattering picture, but probably useful enough for the police. They never managed to catch up with him however, until one month after the failed rising.

Six weeks after Robert's return from France, his father, Dr Robert Emmet, died at "Casino" on December 9, 1802. His mother died the following year while her youngest son was in custody awaiting his trial, on September 9, 1803. Both were buried in St Peter's Churchyard, Aungier Street.

One of the early biographies of Emmet was written by Louise de Broglie, Comtesse d'Haussonville and published in Paris in 1858. She was a grand-daughter of the famous Madame de Staël (Germaine Necker 1766-1817), one of the great intellectuals of her time, whose salon in Paris was famous as a meeting place for writers and thinkers of the revolutionary and romantic period.

The Comtesse had another profile to offer, based no doubt on what Madame de Staël had told her family of the young Emmet she knew in Paris:

"He was above the middle stature, rather slight and delicate, although endowed with nervous strength which enabled him to support great fatigue. He walked with a quick step, and all his movements were rapid. The portraits remaining of him have been made after his death, and the painter, it is said, preoccupied with his tragic fate, has given him a sad sombre expression which he had not in the happy days of life. His countenance was pleasing and *distingué*. His hair was brown and his complexion quite pale; the eyebrow was arched, and the eyes black and large with dark eye-lashes, which gave to his looks a remarkable expression of pride, penetration, and mildness. His nose was aquiline and his mouth was slightly disdainful.

"Energy, delicacy, and tenderness are expressed in his melancholy and ardent features. Such was, however, his total absence of affectation and his simplicity, that modesty of his character, joined to a sort of habitual reserve, hid the working of his mind in the ordinary circumstances of life, but, were any subject started which was deeply interesting to him, he appeared quite another man."

CHAPTER THREE

⟫◆⟪

IN THE "CASINO" home and grounds in Milltown Robert had constructed an elaborate system of tunnels and secret passages, where he could hide and effect his escape into the countryside. When Dr Richard Madden, historian of the United Irishmen, visited the house in 1836 it was in the possession of a Mr George Stapleton. Madden spoke to two of Dr Emmet's faithful servants, one of whom was the gardener in 1803. Madden describes what he found:

"In the ceiling, over the passage leading from the hall-door towards the kitchen, he pointed out to me the place where the boards overhead were sawed through; the square portion thus cut was sufficiently large to allow a person to pass through when the boards were removed, which formed the trap-door communicating from the upper part of the house to the hall. If attention had not been directed to it, no one would have observed the cutting in the boards. On the ground floor, on the left-hand side of the hall, there is a small room adjoining the kitchen, which was called 'Master Robert's bedroom'."

Later still, in 1880, Dr TA Emmet, Robert's grand-nephew, visited the house and reported as follows:

> "The appearance of the house and grounds was essentially the same as when occupied by the family, with the single exception that the window-frames in the front of the house having become decayed, new ones fitted with plate glass had been substituted for old.
>
> "The garden had been preserved just as Dr Emmet had laid it out, for when the greenhouses had been decayed new ones in facsimile had been put in their place. The wall-fruit, too, which the doctor had planted and trailed, was all preserved by building new trellis about it where necessary. It was stated that even the vegetables were of the same stock as had been found on the place, and occupied the same locality. The parlour was still covered by the tapestry paper

as of old, which, no doubt, had been a source of delight to the younger generation of the past."

Robert's escape tunnel ran from beneath two basement windows to a summer house situated fifty yards away and apparently he had reason to use this tunnel on more than one occasion.

Planning and preparation took up almost all of Emmet's time now, gradually becoming more particular, focused and detailed. This was no one-man band, however. The organisers included many men of undoubted ability and commitment,

As well as Thomas Russell, there was Miles Byrne of Monaseed, Co Wexford who had fought in 1798 and who later had a distinguished career in the army of France. He did not die until 1862 and his *Memoirs*, which are an invaluable source of information, were published posthumously by his wife in 1863.

Miles Byrne was a power of strength and intellect and he gave all the assistance he could. He thought Emmet's plan was an excellent one. As well as reaching the grade of Chef de Bataillon or Colonel in the French army he was awarded the Cross of the Légion d'Honneur and the St Helena Medal before he retired. After the failed Rising Emmet had sent him to France to seek assistance once more.

Others involved were James Hope who had fought in the Battle of Antrim in 1798; Michael Dwyer, who was still conducting his guerrilla campaign against the Crown Forces in the Wicklow Mountains; John Allen, a woollen draper in Dublin; Philip Long, a general merchant in Dublin; Denis Lambert Redmond, a coal merchant in Dublin; William Henry Hamilton, a lawyer in Enniskillen; John Stockdale, a Dublin printer; Nicholas Stafford, a baker in James's Street, and many others.

An analysis and critical assessment of the failure of the 1798 Rising had been carried out by the surviving leaders during 1799. This enquiry revealed two major deficiencies: they had been infiltrated by government agents, and this infiltration had been possible due to the fact that the United Irishmen were a mass, loosely organised movement. The second weakness was a lack of discipline, which some commentators even described as a descent into licentiousness on the part of some of the insurgents. There is no doubt but that excessive consumption of alcohol by men on active service was a gross imprudence, and that those in charge often failed to grapple and cope with this indiscipline.

The ascending structure of the movement had been such that the lower ranks elected the superior committees, and the new leadership decided to change that around. A more secretive organisation was developed. An elite group at the top handpicked the officers in a descending order; the generals carefully handpicked the colonels and so on down.

Security was now of the utmost importance, to the extent that the lower ranks would be filled only at the last moment; there would be no more than twenty-fours' notice of mobilisation; instructions would be transmitted by word of mouth; and arms would not be distributed until the last moment.

All of this planning was based, not only on a realistic assessment of previous shortcomings, but also on the expectation of French assistance and the assumption that there was still in Ireland a broad mass of people who were ready to rise again. This new approach called for new skills and talents, however, and these were not always available. The effort to steer clear of spies and informers was undoubtedly successful, but the major changes in organisation which were adopted to achieve this brought other problems in their train.

Emmet's Proclamation announced the existence of a Provisional Government, but did not give their names. William Wickham, the Chief Secretary stated afterwards that, along with Emmet, Russell, Hamilton, Long, Allen, Murphy (a Dublin tailor) and Byrne were "the very life and soul of the treason".

The seizure of Dublin Castle was pivotal to the overall plan as adopted, it would be the psychological trigger which would rouse the country, and Emmet, the energetic, optimistic, educated member of a respected family, who had been to France and knew the situation there, was the obvious man to take charge in Dublin. As things turned out, he became the Commander in Chief.

Finance, as ever, was important. More than that, it was a problem. There were well-to-do acquaintances who would encourage revolutionaries, but talk is cheap. When approached for a subscription, many of them just faded from view. The workers and tradesmen could contribute little. Philip Long, the merchant in Crow Street, seems to have contributed money generously, in the region of £1,400. The main source of funds was Dr Emmet's last will and testament. He left £2,000 to Robert, a considerable sum, worth more than €100,000 in today's money, and every penny of it was spent in the cause of Irish freedom.

Miles Byrne wrote many years later:

"Mr Emmet's powerful, persuasive language, and sound reason, all coming from the heart, left it impossible for any Irishman, impressed with a desire for his country's independence, to make any objection to his plans (particularly as Ireland's great opportunity seemed now to have arrived for her freedom), save to bide the proper time, and wait for French aid. For my own part, I had no objections to make. I merely observed that I trusted the poor county of Wexford, and the other parts which suffered in 1798, would be spared until Dublin was ready to begin and take the lead in the struggle; that for the accomplishment of this enterprise there were more than three hundred brave county of Wexford fellows who escaped in '98 and who took refuge in Dublin and the environs, on whom we could count when the time for action arrived, and that with the aid of those tried men, and with the brave Kildare men and Dublin citizens, I trusted success was certain.

"We settled in this first interview how we were to meet."

It is important to appreciate that Emmet did not trust Bonaparte and he was disturbed at French interventions in Switzerland, Holland and Italy. Nevertheless, he regarded French military assistance, in both men and materials, as important, but the French role was to be a supportive one. They would come as auxiliaries, just as they had helped the American War of Independence. A Provisional Government was established and Ireland would not swap one tyranny for another.

Emmet was inclined to favour the George Washington model in America, and sought an alliance and a guarantee from the French, such as Benjamin Franklin, as Ambassador to France, had negotiated. France would help to separate Ireland from England, but Ireland would be free and sovereign.

CHAPTER 4

⎯⎯⬦⬦⎯⎯

THE TIMING OF A RISING has always been a tricky problem. When is too early, when would turn out to be too late, and when could the organisers take optimum advantage of all the factors and circumstances? There is a Greek word called "kairos" which means "the appropriate or opportune time". In Irish we have the words "uain" and "ionú", more precise terms than "am", or "tráth". For Pearse and Connolly and their comrades, Easter 1916 was "the right moment to reveal itself".

A premature strike would be unwise, but by waiting too long opportunities might pass and disappear. The United Irishmen hesitated in 1796-98, in a quandary between striking first and then getting French assistance or awaiting a French landing and then taking to the field. This same factor came into play again, but Emmet had seen and heard enough in Paris to be of the opinion that they could not count on a French force coming.

The renewal of the war between France and England, was, however, an important factor. So also was the resultant panic in England as they feared an invasion by Bonaparte; as was, from a security point of view, the arrest and execution of Colonel Despard and his followers, because Despard's plans were linked to Ireland and to Emmet through William Dowdall. The resumed war would also entail the withdrawal of troops from Ireland. All of these factors seemed to indicate that an earlier rather than a later date would be more advantageous.

A significant factor in all of this is the organisation, training and readiness of one's own forces, as well as adequate arms, supplies and equipment.

On April 23, 1803 Emmet leased a house in Butterfield Lane, Rathfarnham, under the name of Robert Ellis, and from this point on the preparations for the rising occupied all his time. He did not even bother to furnish this house which was now the centre for planning operations. When Michael Dwyer, Miles Byrne and other Wicklow and Wexford leaders visited him everybody slept on mattresses on the floor. He remained indoors by day, visitors came after dark and meetings were held at night.

Anne Devlin, a first cousin of Michael Dwyer through her mother, and who was a daughter of Brian Devlin who had a dairy farm nearby, kept house. She was not just a servant though. She was a trusted courier and confidante, a comrade in revolution who was utterly faithful until her death in 1851.

Anne Devlin

It was less than five years since the 1798 Rising had been brutally suppressed and now already a new leadership was emerging. Michael Dwyer was still attacking and harassing the enemy from time to time and fading into the shelter of his beautiful Wicklow Mountains and of his beloved trustworthy people. Miles Byrne was a skilled soldier and leader of men. Contact had been re-established with the North through James Hope and Thomas Russell. Both were well respected among the United Irishmen in Antrim and Down. Soon the plans to strike another blow and establish an Irish Republic were taking shape.

Depots were established in Dublin for the manufacture and storage of war materials. Some of these were within half a mile of Dublin Castle itself, at Marshalsea Lane (Thomas Street), Patrick Street, Winetavern Street (in the vault of a disused inn opposite Christchurch). There were other depots in Irishtown (Ringsend) and across the Liffey in Smithfield.

Marshalsea Lane, known locally as Mass Lane, was in the area of the brewing trade, as it still is, next door to the Guinness brewery. Emmet got the use of a large disused malt house at the rear of an inn called the White Bull and kept by a Mrs Dillon. The main entrance was from Marshalsea Lane, but there was a private entrance from the inn. A small band of no more than forty skilled and trusted men worked by day and night in these depots.

Marianne Elliott in *Partners in Revolution* gives an idea of the amount of work done:

> "On the night of 23 July when the military reached the Marshalsea Lane depot, they found their way blocked by a solid wall of pikes, let down from the depot's hatch for

transportation to the scene of action. Inside they found enough ammunition for 10,000 men and about 7,000 additional pikes behind a false wall."

The Patrick Street depot had a system of secret passages similar to those constructed at "Casino". A timber merchant called Thomas Branagan was in charge of the Irishtown depot. Together, he and Emmet took plans of the Pigeon House Fort from Sandymount Strand and tested some of Emmet's newly-developed rockets there. Within and between the depots a secret communication system was devised and operated by using specially marked ivory counters and tokens.

Dublin city at that time had all the principal streets that it still has, but it also had a maze of side streets, back streets, lanes and alleys. There were numerous blacksmiths' workshops and other premises where iron and metal works, as well as other trades were carried on. The nearest thing to it nowadays would be some of the small workshops for motor repairs and spraying, where one could also bring a lawnmower or even a television set for attention.

Tunnels, secret passages, trap doors, scaling ladders and rockets were not the only artefacts of Emmet's creative genius. He experimented with chemicals and explosives and developed a jointed or folding pike which could be carried unobtrusively from place to place under a greatcoat. In the depots they manufactured ammunition, hand grenades, fuses, rockets and musket balls. The signal for the Rising was to be given by the firing of a rocket which could be seen from various points in the city.

It was in the Patrick Street depot that a former soldier with the East India Company, a Scotsman called Johnstone, pooled his practical rocket expertise with the scientific knowledge Emmet had brought home from France. Together they devised an improved device. This was the forerunner of what was later known as the Congreve rocket. The British were also seeking to develop effective rockets. They captured some from Emmet's arsenal after the Rising and they offered one of the Republicans, a man called Finnerty, freedom from prosecution and almost certain execution if he would go to England to work for them. He agreed and was sent to the Royal Arsenal in Woolwich and there he contributed to William Congreve's work. The famous Congreve rocket was in fact a further refinement of Emmet's rocket.

Emmet also devised an ingenious method of transporting weapons from place to place by means of hollowed beams of wood. He had other beams hollowed out and filled with explosives, with fuses attached. These beams were mounted on wheels for easier and faster dispatch in launching them against the enemy.

Miles Byrne gives a detailed description of some of these newly-developed instruments of war and recounts how they went out one day to a quiet field beyond Rathfarnham to try out a new rocket or flame thrower:

> "The rocket was made fast to a pole with wire, and rested on a trestle; the match being put to it, it went off like a thunderbolt, carrying the pole along with it, and throwing flames and fire behind, as it advanced; and when it fell, it went on tearing up the ground till the last of the matter with which it was filled was completely consumed."

The 1798 insurgents were at a disadvantage when the enemy had artillery and they had none. Rockets of this nature would have created havoc in enemy lines.

Plans were also made to cover the bridges over the Liffey (not as many then as now) with boards, full of long nails, bound at each end with iron bars which had eighteen-inch spikes in them. These spikes would be hammered into the roadway and the nailed boards would impede a column of infantry or cavalry. While Dublin Castle was the main target, barracks on the south side would be attacked. Enemy reinforcements from the north side would be delayed while seized arms and stores would be quickly distributed, even as far as Wicklow. There were many surprises in store for the forces of the Crown.

The Dublin plan counted on the availability of 300 Kildare men, 300 Wexford men and 200 Wicklow men, as well as many United Men in Dublin itself, possibly numbering up to 3,000, according to some accounts. This was apparently scaled down, and the attack on the Castle with a small force became the main focus. This Castle had been the seat of English power for six centuries. Previous patriots like Seán Mór Ó Néill, Eoghan Rua Ó Néill and others had all attempted to seize it. Pearse and Connolly did likewise in 1916.

In terms of timing, everything was being put in place for a strike later in the year.

CHAPTER 5

⟫◦⟪

DURING THESE MOMENTOUS EVENTS the Lord Lieutenant, who resided in the Viceregal Lodge in the Phoenix Park, was Lord Hardwicke. His Chief Secretary was William Wickham and the Under-Secretary was Alexander Marsden. General Henry Fox had been appointed Commander of His Majesty's Forces in Ireland in May, 1802, but he seems to have been more concerned about a possible French invasion than an insurrection in Ireland itself.

Reports coming into the Castle from various parts of the country indicated that there was little or no evidence of rebellion. Emmet was awaiting the withdrawal of more English troops from Dublin to serve in the renewed war with France. His hand was forced however by an unfortunate accident on the evening of Saturday, July 16. There was an explosion of gunpowder in the Patrick Street depot, and one of the men, John Keenan, bled to death as a result. His brother, Thomas Keenan, was later hanged on September 11 for his involvement in the Rising.

The police arrived at the depot, but everything of a suspicious nature seems to have been carefully tidied away. It is not clear from accounts whether Major Sirr and Under-Secretary Marsden took this matter seriously. In all events there was no general roundup of suspects. Marsden was given a report on the incident by Major Sirr. *Habeas Corpus* was not suspended at that time, and Marsden explained afterwards that they had not ordered a search for arms because "the alarm attending it would have been exceedingly great, and the event might not have justified such a very strong measure".

It is difficult to escape the conclusion that even if there had been no treachery in the Republican ranks up to that point, the Castle authorities must have been on alert after the accident in Patrick Street. The following Saturday, July 23 was set as the date for the Rising. Russell, Hope and Hamilton were dispatched to the North to organise their men. Dublin would rise first and the North would follow. Emmet hoped that on hearing of the successful seizure of power in Dublin eighteen other counties would rise. Apart from Kildare, Wicklow, Wexford, Antrim and Down, counties with which we know he was in direct and constant contact, it is now impossible to say what other areas he had in mind. We must ask ourselves if he was over-optimistic to the point of being unrealistic.

Such was the discontent of the people, there is no doubt that if power were seized in Dublin and the Leinster and Ulster counties rose, the rest of Ireland would follow. The militia were the weak link in the Crown forces and Republican successes would have undermined their allegiance. This had happened in Castlebar in 1798 when the Longford and Kilkenny militias changed sides almost en masse.

A limited number of trusted officers were told of the new date. Miles Byrne and Michael Quigley were given instructions as to mobilisation of the Dublin men. During the week pikes were distributed to safe houses throughout the city. This was all done under the very noses of the police.

Patrick M Geoghegan, in his book *Robert Emmet, A Life* (2002), says that "the plan for taking Dublin was breathtaking in its precision and audacity. It was nothing less than an ambitious blueprint for a dramatic *coup d'état*."

Initially, barracks at the Pigeon House, Island Bridge and Cork Street were to be attacked. Emmet himself would lead the main attack on the seat of power, Dublin Castle. Other targets were the Royal Barracks (now Collins Barracks) and the Old Custom House Barracks near the bottom of Parliament Street.

In these attacks, sentries would be overpowered if possible, groups of men would climb the walls using the scaling ladders, and arms would be seized, including artillery. Houses in the vicinity of these positions were to be taken over. Where an attack might fail the barracks would be blockaded and entrenchments thrown up against them. Obstructions of every kind would be erected in the streets.

British military headquarters were located in Kilmainham, the centre of administration was in the Castle and the Lord Lieutenant resided in the Phoenix Park. Special attention would be given to impeding communications between these three centres of power. All bridges across the River Liffey would be blocked with the boards full of long nails.

For the attack on the Castle, six coaches were to be commandeered. They would leave Thomas Street at eleven o'clock at night, six men in each coach, each of them carrying a blunderbuss and a folding pike under his great coat. Emmet himself would be one of them. They would gain access to the Castle yard on the pretext of going to a party.

Miles Byrne was to have a detachment of men in Denis Lambert

Redmond's house on Coal Quay (now Wood Quay), and as soon as the last coach passed they would move in quickly behind them. The coaches would enter the Castle first. When Byrne's pikemen reached the Castle immediately after them they would surprise and disarm the guard and substitute their own men for them. A second assault would be launched from a house in Ship Street at the other side of the Castle, at the same time as the attack at the main gate.

The overall plan was divided into three parts, what Emmet called lines of attack, points of check and lines of defence. Geoghegan has commented that "it was an extraordinary revolutionary programme, fully justifying Emmet's reputation for military planning... combining elements of guerrilla warfare and street fighting".

But he remarks that it depended crucially on two factors: arms and men. When the time came he had not sufficient of either. There were plenty of pikes, but a grave shortage of muskets and blunderbusses.

James (Jemmy) Hope

CHAPTER 6

—◆—

S OLID, LEVEL-HEADED MEN like Miles Byrne and Thomas Russell endorsed Emmet's plans for insurrection; seizing Dublin Castle; attacking barracks, mostly on the south side of the Liffey; impeding enemy reinforcements from the north side; sending emissaries to Ulster to prepare for the men of the North to take the field – all of this made sense as a plan on paper.

One hundred and twelve years later when Joseph Mary Plunkett and the Military Council of the Irish Republican Brotherhood were planning the 1916 Rising they studied Emmet's plan and kept it in mind when making their own. Decades earlier, Miles Byrne had written that "his (Emmet's) plans will ever be considered by all those wishing for the independence of poor Ireland."

But, as happened so often in Irish history, as in other countries also, a combination of events and human frailties resulted in confusion and failure on July 23, 1803. We recall that Napoleon Bonaparte, one of the greatest generals in history, always inquired if an officer was lucky. Luck has its own part to play in all human endeavours. The 1916 Rising was planned for Easter Sunday, was called off by Eoin Mac Néill and then hastily rescheduled for Monday, in Dublin at any rate. It nearly did not happen at all.

Leon Ó Broin called his biography *The Unfortunate Mr Robert Emmet* and one can understand why when one considers the genius of the man, the well-laid plans and then the series of mishaps which led to disaster, the execution of 22 Republicans and the jailing of many more, including members of Emmet's own extended family.

It is not easy to recount or describe what happened on that fateful day, but we can try. It was a Saturday. Emmet had slept the Friday night in the Thomas Street depot. When he got up he went on horseback to Butterfield Lane. There he bade goodbye to Anne Devlin and asked her brother Arthur to send a message to Michael Dwyer to assemble his Wicklow men and make for Dublin. Whatever messenger was sent delayed on his journey and Dwyer did not get the message until Sunday. This was the beginning of the unravelling of the plan.

On returning to Thomas Street, Emmet found that several people had converged on the depot and were getting in the way of the workmen who were striving to have everything ready in time. A good officer on the spot would not have allowed this to happen.

Three hundred men had been requested from Kildare but many more than that turned up in the morning, coming in along the Naas Road and some by canal barge, which brought them quite close to the centre of operations. This was almost too good and was not managed properly. It was a warm summer day and the Rising was timed for the evening. The men could not be assembled in one or two places without arousing suspicion, so they spread out around the city and inevitably drank a lot in the pubs.

The Kildare men were not impressed by Emmet – he was young and average in stature, no Kelly from Killanne. Some of them asked to see what arms were available and two of them were brought to Thomas Street, by now a centre of confusion, and shown the jointed pikes and explosive beams. They wanted blunderbusses and muskets. Emmet set about getting £500 from Philip Long, the merchant in Crow Street to buy more blunderbusses. The Kildare men were not impressed, were unsure of the wisdom of going ahead without a precise date for a French landing and began to drift away home from the city.

Then a rumour was spread among the Dublin men that the Rising had been postponed until the following Wednesday. Emmet got a report that a Mr Edward Clarke of Palmerstown, a justice of the peace who employed 300 men in a cotton factory, had been to the Castle to warn the authorities that something was afoot. In fact this man had been to see Alexander Marsden, the Under-Secretary, earlier in the week but his warning was not taken seriously. On the Saturday, some of his workmen who were United Men had told Clarke that they were going into the city to take part in a rising and they wanted their wages before they left! This would have sounded so ridiculous, so preposterous and unbelievable, that it was probably not taken seriously.

On receipt of this latest information, Emmet took precautionary measures. He sent some men to patrol the roads between the Royal Barracks and British Army HQ in Kilmainham and to impede any communication between either place and the Castle. He stationed guards around the store and explosive beams were issued to hinder any pre-emptive enemy advance on them.

The misfortunes and misadventures were multiplying however, and things were beginning to get out of control. There were not enough blunderbusses, the fuses for the grenades were lost, and only one scaling ladder was completed. Yet, because he had alerted the other counties and because he still held the advantage of surprise, Emmet refused to postpone the Rising.

Shortly after seven o'clock he stood in his green and gold general's uniform in the Thomas Street depot and to a hushed assembly of his men he read aloud the proclamation he had written. The Irish nation was about to assert itself in arms against foreign rule once again. It was a historic moment.

Edmund Condon was in charge of the provision of coaches for the attack on the Castle, but this operation soon ran into trouble. An army officer stopped them and demanded to know what he was doing with so many coaches. Condon pretended he was hard of hearing and drew close to the officer, who became quite menacing. Condon drew his pistol and fired on the officer. The coachmen took fright and made off. Emmet decided that the attack would proceed nevertheless.

Then Michael Quigley rushed into the depot and disclosed that soldiers were bearing down on them. This was not true, but Emmet decided that they were not going to be butchered inside the premises and he gave the order for operations to begin. Pikes were thrown out of the upper window and men in the pubs in the vicinity hurried out. The pre-arranged rocket signal does not appear to have been given.

There was confusion outside on the street, among a disorganised mass of men on a Saturday night. Pikes were distributed and unfortunately the mob joined in. Nowadays, we speak of Murphy's Law, anything that can go wrong sometimes does go wrong. It certainly did on this occasion.

Into all this confusion on Thomas Street a couple of coaches were being driven with some difficulty through the crowd. A man was hauled from the first coach and piked. In the second coach was none other than Lord Kilwarden, Chief Justice, his daughter and his nephew. Kilwarden was on his way from his residence at Newlands, to a meeting of the Privy Council, without an armed escort.

He called out: "It's I, Kilwarden, Chief Justice of the King's Bench". The story is possibly true, possibly not, that a man in the crowd replied: "You're the very man I want," and he piked him. Kilwarden and his nephew were pulled from the coach and killed. Someone, possibly one of Emmet's officers, came on the scene and escorted the young lady from the coach to safety.

This was the same Kilwarden (Arthur Wolfe) who had issued the writ of *habeas corpus* when Wolfe Tone was under sentence of death in 1798. He had shown a certain amount of courage on that occasion but had failed to ensure that his writ would be obeyed. He had been Attorney-General in 1797 when a Co Antrim Presbyterian, William Orr, the first republican martyr, was unjustly put on trial and executed.

It was only a couple of days later that Emmet heard of the death of Kilwarden and his nephew. This and other random acts on that Saturday were not the insurrection he had envisaged. His Proclamation had declared:

"We call upon you… carefully avoiding all appearance of intoxication, plunder or revenge, recollecting that you lost Ireland before, not from want of courage but from not having that courage rightly directed by discipline."

The Volunteers of 1916 prayed that no one would dishonour the cause "by cowardice, inhumanity or rapine". Even the Proclamation of 1916 had echoes of Emmet's Proclamation. It was certainly shorter and more to the point.

Finally, Emmet's force of 80 men who were to take the Castle, had dwindled to about 20. He decided to terminate operations and leave the city, so with a few of his trusted men they retreated through Francis Street and Kevin Street towards Rathfarnham.

There was a skirmish between an armed crowd who attacked a company of the 21st Regiment at the corner of Thomas Street and drove them back towards the James's Street barracks, killing one soldier. Six or seven of the crowd were killed and some prisoners taken. The Coombe barracks was also attacked about 11.30 but the military repulsed the attackers, killing four and wounding many more. For the British it was now a mopping-up operation.

There had also been some minor skirmishes in various parts of the city, as well as in Rathcoole, Maynooth, Celbridge, Chapelizod and Naas, which shows that there was fairly substantial mobilisation, but by midnight it was all over.

The English authorities began a search for the leaders and participants in the Rising. Among the Crown Forces was the Lawyers' Corps of Loyal Yeomen, which included in its ranks one Daniel O'Connell from Derrynane, Co Kerry. Each member was ordered to give three days service, but the 'liberator' volunteered for a further period of three days, so great was his enthusiasm for bringing rebels to 'justice'. After that he frequently condemned the United Irishmen during his long career as a lawyer and politician.

But, if Emmet's Rising degenerated into confusion, the people on the other side had their problems too. Marsden, in the Castle, had plenty of intelligence reports, not from within Republican ranks as far as we know, but of a general nature. At 2pm he told Maj-Gen Sir Charles Asgill, Commander of the Dublin District, that he had "reason to think that something serious is intended". This would have been based on various intelligence reports, such

Thomas Russell

as an unusually high number of men moving into Dublin along the Naas
Road. There was never any shortage of informers, loyal or otherwise, who
kept the Castle supplied with information if anything suspicious seemed
to be stirring. They were well paid for their work, and the more useful
information they brought the more they were paid.

Marsden sent a message to Hardwicke, the Lord Lieutenant and asked him
to come to the Castle, and bring the GOC, General Fox, with him. They
both arrived at the Castle at 3.15pm. Marsden put it to Fox that immediate
defensive measures should be taken – reinforce the Pigeon House defences,
double the guard on the arms magazine in the Phoenix Park, and so on.
Hardwicke wanted the Bank of Ireland protected. Fox apparently showed an
appalling ignorance of the geography of Dublin city. It was also discovered
afterwards that there were no supplies of ammunition in the Castle.

Fox returned to his headquarters at the Royal Hospital in Kilmainham, at
4.30pm. He sent a message to Colonel Vassal, field officer of the day, to call

on him at 9.30pm, after his dinner, no doubt. When Vassal called, he told him that the people in the Castle were expecting a rising, but that he himself did not believe it. Hardwicke had assumed that the GOC would have put the whole garrison an alert, but he did no such thing until it was too late.

General Fox displayed extraordinary ineptitude. If only Emmet had had his arms and his men, including good quality officers, he could well have seized the Castle and taken control of the city. In these circumstances, the other counties would have risen in support.

"Had I another week, had I one thousand pounds, had I one thousand men, I would have feared nothing," he wrote afterwards.

Miles Byrne wrote afterwards in his *Memoirs*:

> "... the Castle would have been surprised and taken, the Government being then completely off its guard. Once in possession of it, the citizens en masse would have flocked to the standard of independence hoisted on this monument, the emblem of Ireland's degradation for centuries... A few hours would have sufficed to dislodge the English garrison of Dublin, who mustered weaker than at any other time... and by threatening to set fire to those quarters where resistance was made, the troops defending them would have been soon forced to capitulate. Not for centuries had Ireland so favourable an opportunity of getting rid of the cruel English yoke..."

When it came to the blame game in the weeks that followed, why the Dublin garrison of 3,000 troops should have been in such a state of unreadiness, why this conspiracy had got so far without being discovered, the spotlight was turned on General Fox. He was later relieved of his position and posted to Sicily.

CHAPTER 7

—————≫◆≪—————

Emmet retreated to Butterfield Lane with about a dozen of his men. Anne Devlin was there to receive them and she is reported to have censured them for their failure.

"Bad welcome to you", she said. "Is the world lost by you, you cowards that you are, to lead the people to destruction, and then to leave them." "Don't blame me", said Emmet, "the fault is not mine".

The company moved on the next day to the house of the farmer called "Silky" Johnny Doyle at Ballymace, Tallaght and again to the house of a woman called Rose Bagenall at Ballynascorny.

The police found letters in the Thomas Street depot which led them to Butterfield Lane, Rathfarnham, in a search for "Mr Ellis". They arrived on Monday, July 25, but as Sirr remarked he had found the nest, but the bird had flown. The twenty-five year old Anne Devlin was there on her own. They demanded to know who Mr Ellis was and who were the men who had been staying with him.

Anne responded with extraordinary fortitude and courage, with real heroism. She just repeated: "I have nothing to tell. I'll tell you nothing". The magistrate in charge ordered the Yeomen to half hang her. They took a sidecar and placed it with the shafts in the air.

While the makeshift gallows was being prepared, Anne was forced to stand with her back to the wall. The soldiers prodded her with bayonets until she was covered in blood. They demanded information and she still refused to tell them. They then put a rope around her and brought her to the gallows.

The question was put one last time. "Now, will you tell us where Mr Ellis is?" She refused in these words: "You can kill me, you blackguards, but as much as one word you won't get from me about him". The rope was pulled and Anne was suspended in mid-air for a minute or two. They then let her down, loosened the rope and went off with themselves. Anne recovered from this terrible ordeal.

Dr Madden describes a visit he paid to the Butterfield Lane house many years later:

"In the summer of 1843, accompanied by Anne Devlin, I proceeded to Butterfield Lane to ascertain the fact of the existence or non-existence of the house in which Robert Emmet had resided for some months in 1803. For a length of time our search was fruitless. The recollection of a locality at the expiration of forty years is a very dim sort of reminiscence. There was no house in the lane, the exterior of which reminded my conductress of her old scene of suffering. At length her eye caught an old range of buildings at some distance, like the offices of a farmhouse. This she at once recognised as part of the premises of her father, and she soon was able to point out the well known fields around it, which had once been in her father's possession. The house, alongside of which we were standing on the right-hand side of the lane going from Rathfarnham road, she said must be the house of Mr Emmet, though the entrance was entirely altered; however, the position of an adjoining house left little doubt on her mind. We knocked at the door, and I found the house was inhabited by a lady of my acquaintance, the daughter of a Protestant clergyman, who had been, strange to say, the college friend and most intimate acquaintance of Robert Emmet, the late Dr Hayden, of Rathcoole.

"The lady of the house, in whom I discovered an acquaintance, left us no doubt on the subject of the locality – we were in the house that had been tenanted by Robert Emmet. The scene that ensued is one more easily conceived than described. We were conducted over the house – my aged companion at first in silence, and then, as if slowly awakening from a dream, rubbing her dim eyes, and here and there pausing for some moments when she came to some recognised spot. On the ground floor she pointed out a small room, on the left-hand of the entrance – 'That's the room where Mr Dowdall and Mr Hamilton used to sleep.' The entrance had been changed from about the centre to the right-hand end; the window of a small room there had been converted into the door-way, and the room itself into the hall. 'This,' said Anne Devlin, 'was my room; I know it well – my mattress used to be in that corner.' There was one place, every corner and cranny of which she seemed to have a familiar acquaintance with, and that was the kitchen. On the upper floor, the principal bedroom at the present time attracted her particular attention; she stood for some time gazing into the room from the doorway; I asked her whose room it had been. It was a good while before I got an answer in words, but her trembling hands, and the few tears which came from a deep source, and spoke of sorrow of an old date, left no necessity to repeat the question – it was the room of Robert Emmet."

Meanwhile, Emmet had gone on into the Wicklow Mountains. Miles Byrne states in his *Memoirs*:

"Both Mr John Patten and Mr Philip Long endeavoured to persuade Emmet of the urgent necessity of his going at once to France; to which he replied that it should never be said of him that he had abandoned the brave people implicated through his means."

Emmet himself thought that Byrne should go to France.

On the following Saturday, July 30, Emmet returned to Dublin to a safe house he had used previously, Palmer's in Harold's Cross, using the name of Mr Hewitt. This house was located on the main road, between the Grand Canal and Mount Drummond Avenue.

He stayed in this house for the best part of a month. Miles Byrne came to see him, as did Philip Long, and John Patten who was Thomas Addis's brother-in-law. Anne Devlin brought letters and took others away. Some of this correspondence was with Sarah Curran.

Byrne describes how they discussed what went wrong on July 23. He wrote his *Memoirs* towards the end of his long life, probably fifty or more years after these events. Given his distinguished military career in France it is reasonable to conclude that he was used to writing precise and correct reports for his superiors. His evidence on the events of 1798 and 1803 is vital to our understanding of all that happened then.

Regarding the evening of the Rising, July 23, 1803 he says that he told Emmet when he met him in Palmer's house in Harold's Cross, that he had assembled his men at Redmond's house on the Coal Quay at seven o'clock.

One of his men passed through the Castle yard at 8.45 – entering at Ship Street and leaving through the main gate. He reported that everything was quiet.

He later sent a trusted man called Pat Ford to Thomas Street to confirm that they were ready. This man never returned. Fearing that he had been arrested he sent another man called Terence Kavanagh as a second messenger. He came back and reported the confusion and disasters which had occurred. On hearing this, Byrne and his men quit the house and withdrew through Nicholas Street, Patrick Street and New Street. They marched and countermarched in search of Emmet and his men. In doing this, their pikes would have been concealed of course and they would have kept to a loose though disciplined formation. They separated before daylight and went to ground.

Byrne further records Emmet's own report, telling how the six coaches were lost. These are Emmet's words as recorded by Byrne:

> "Condon seeing them drive off, returned to tell me what had happened to him. I then decided that the men who were to be conveyed in the coaches should go on foot to the Castle, and whilst preparing for this march, a false alarm was given that troops were surrounding the depot and in consequence our men there began to rush out, too hurriedly no doubt, and by the time they got to Thomas Street, disorder and confusion got amongst them. You heard of course what happened there, after which an attack on the Castle could not be thought of; consequently the signal rockets were not made use of."

These are Emmet's own words as quoted by a professional military officer, Miles Byrne. "I could see plainly," he adds, "how he was overwhelmed with sorrow whilst speaking on this sad subject."

Byrne is very critical of William Dowdall for failing to preserve discipline and prevent the disasters and false alarm, but he offers no evidence for mentioning this man in particular. He then adds that he cannot give an opinion on others, "not knowing their engagements with Mr Emmet, but their absence was a cruel loss, for amongst them were the bravest of the brave, who would have made the men observe order in their march to the Castle, which would have been surprised and taken, the Government being then completely off its guard . . ."

Byrne concludes this part of his *Memoirs* as follows:

> "I took my last farewell of this magnanimous young man, who during this interview never uttered a word of blame against any of those leaders who might have preserved discipline and prevented the disasters and false alarms which produced such bad effects on the men in Thomas Street."

Byrne did go to Paris to see Thomas Addis Emmet. He never saw Ireland again, but as noted earlier, he had a distinguished career in the army of France and wrote his *Memoirs*, which are a most valuable source of information on the events of 1798 and 1803. He died in January 24, 1862. There is a Celtic cross over his grave in Montmartre Cemetery in Paris and the inscription on it is in French and Irish.

Whilst in Palmer's Emmet heard that a relative of his, St John Mason, had been arrested, as well as Philip Long, and also Anne Devlin.

Anne was taken to the Castle and Major Sirr tried to break her. She was offered £500, an enormous sum at that time which Sirr described as "a fine fortune for a young woman". She never flinched, never yielded. She was transferred to Kilmainham Jail and put in solitary confinement.

During the time he was in Harold's Cross Emmet arranged to communicate with his ailing mother and to meet Sarah Curran. His mother advised him to leave Ireland. He had developed and practised different styles of handwriting, so as to confuse the authorities if any of his letters was intercepted. Sarah Curran urged him to destroy letters she had sent him, but he did not do so. Two of these letters are still extant.

By this time the authorities had offered a reward of £300 for the arrest of Robert Emmet and £1,000 for information leading to the arrest of the killers of Lord Kilwarden. Every householder was ordered to affix to the hall-door a list of the occupants.

On the evening of Thursday, August 25 Major Sirr raided the Palmer house and Emmet was arrested, although Sirr was not quite sure he had the right man. It is assumed that an informer had betrayed him, but that informer may just have been a nosy neighbour who was suspicious and who did not really know the identity of the gentleman who was staying at Palmer's.

Dr Richard Madden draws attention to the Secret Service money report for 1803 which includes the following entry:

"Nov 1, Finlay & Co, account of Richard Jones £1,000 0s 0d."

Madden's view is that this was a reward paid for the arrest of Robert Emmet. Finlay & Co was a bank and the account holder was Richard Jones. The money was probably to be passed by him to the informer.

The historian adds: "The circumstance of lodging the money in this case in the hands of a banker leads to the conclusion that the informer was not a person in an humble rank of life."

Sirr put a guard an Emmet, who gave his name as Cunningham and said he came from Co Wicklow, and the police chief then went back to the canal bridge to bring in his reinforcements. During this couple of minutes Emmet overpowered the guard and made a bid for freedom through the rear of the house. Sirr caught up with him, brought him to the ground and overpowered him. On his person he had two letters from Sarah Curran. Sirr had got his man.

Emmet was brought to the Castle and identified. Dr Madden suggests that the Rev Mr Elrington of TCD, who had previously supplied a description of him, was the one to provide the conclusive identification. Some hours later the prisoner admitted that he was indeed Robert Emmet.

Robert Emmet designed this seal for the United Irishmen.
It depicts a kneeling female playing a harp. The winged maiden on the harp
turns her head to face the player. There is a trophy of arms and armour
in the background, surmounted by a Liberty cap.

CHAPTER 8

⟫⋄⟪

CHIEF SECRETARY WILLIAM WICKHAM had Emmet committed to Kilmainham Jail on the following day, August 26. This jail had been opened in 1796 and was under the governorship of a Mr John Dunn. The Medical Superintendent and Chief Supervisor was a Dr Edward Trevor, a truly cruel and wicked man, who treated prisoners very badly, including Anne Devlin.

The authorities had some difficulty in constructing a case against Emmet, on a charge of high treason. He was a young man of unblemished character who was liked by all who knew him. Even people who deplored his Republicanism were reluctant to testify against him.

Another problem was his handwriting. The State had seized several documents, including proclamations which were regarded as treasonous. But Emmet had developed and practised three or four completely different styles of handwriting. Wickham admitted: "Those who know his handwriting in better days cannot say that they believe the papers of which we are in possession to be written by him."

The two letters from Sarah Curran, which were in his pocket when he was arrested, although unsigned, worried Emmet greatly. He dreaded the thought that he might have incriminated her. Unknown to him, the State did not believe they were love letters at all and thought they were seditious material written in code, possibly by the prisoner's sister, Mary Anne Holmes.

The interrogation of Emmet began on August 30. This was carried out by the Chief Secretary himself, William Wickham, the Attorney-General Standish O'Grady and Lord Redesdale and was called a Privy Council cross-examination. Emmet declined to answer any questions, beyond confirming his name. He was asked about travel to France, about the events of July 23, about the various noms de guerre he had used. He still refused to answer, to confirm or to deny suggestions put to him.

It was when they produced the two letters from Sarah Curran that he began to answer some questions. They frightened him by telling him that these two letters constituted evidence in themselves against the person who wrote them. He feared greatly for Sarah's safety and became quite concerned about his duty to protect her. The chivalrous young man was quite prepared to go to the scaffold to protect the great love of his life.

Emmet had so far managed to hold his own against the questioning. But it was three to one, and the experienced interrogators would have spotted from the change in his demeanour that they had found a weak spot.

An attempt at escape from Kilmainham ended in failure, when one of the warders who agreed to help reported everything to Dr Trevor. Emmet was unaware of this warder's duplicity and he naively entrusted to this man a letter he had written to Sarah Curran, believing that he would have it delivered. Within a few hours this letter was in Wickham's hands and he ordered a search of the Curran home in Rathfarnham the next morning.

When this search took place it was carried out in a very clumsy manner. John Philpot Curran, Sarah's father, was not at home. Sarah herself was still in bed. Major Sirr entered her bedroom and when she realised who he was she became very agitated. In the chaos which followed, her sister Amelia took the love letters from where she kept them and threw them in the fire. The police managed to recover only a few scraps.

Mr Curran was very upset at all of this and had difficulty in persuading the authorities that he knew nothing of his daughter's love affair with Robert Emmet. Wickham decided against prosecuting Sarah, although he did remark that "mademoiselle seems a true pupil of Mary Wollstonecraft". Mary Wollstonecraft was a feminist who belonged to the English Jacobins and had published in 1792 a book entitled *Vindication of the Rights of Women*, in which she demanded equal educational opportunities for women. She also published a vigorous reply to Edmund Burke which she called *View of the French Revolution* (1794). She married the philosopher William Godwin and their daughter Mary married the poet Shelley, who in his turn greatly admired Emmet. (See poem in appendices.)

On the night of that same day on which the Curran home was raided, September 9, Thomas Russell, "the man from God knows where", was captured. He had travelled in an open boat from Bangor in Co Down as far as Drogheda and then came from Drogheda to Dublin where he rented a room at 28 Parliament Street, near the Castle. He was planning to rescue Emmet, but on hearing that there was a reward of £1,500 for his own arrest and on realising that the rescue was a forlorn hope, he decided to make his own escape to the Isle of Man, disguised as a clergyman. Before he could do this, Major Sirr raided the house and arrested him. Suspicion rests on two informers, John Swift Emerson, a lawyer, and Walter Cox, a newspaper editor.

Russell was taken back to Co Down and tried on October 20, in Downpatrick. He was convicted of high treason and hanged the next day. He was buried in Downpatrick Protestant Graveyard and his grave is marked by a stone erected by Mary Ann McCracken, sister of Henry Joy McCracken, bearing the simple inscription, *The Grave of Russell.*

Thomas Russell was a man of great intellectual ability. He became an Ulsterman by adoption. He enjoyed all the discussions and debates about reason, democracy, romanticism, religion and social issues in the Belfast of his time, when that city was known as "the Athens of the North". In 1794 he was appointed librarian of the Linenhall Library there. His *Letter to the people of Ireland on the present situation of the country* in 1796 was used as a pretext to arrest and imprison him. Of the group of prisoners who were released from Fort George in June 1802, he was the one who was the most enthusiastic about reorganising the United movement.

Russell differed from most of the radical French writers of his time, and many of his comrades too, in asserting that Christianity, as he understood it, was really a force for social and political progress. He was of course speaking of the true and original Christianity and not the Church institutions of his time and he saw no incompatibility between the Rights of Man and authentic Christianity. He made a splendid speech from the dock.

Robert Emmet had hoped that John Philpot Curran would defend him, but that was now impossible. Instead, he was defended by Peter Burrowes and Leonard McNally. McNally was mistakenly trusted by the United Irishmen. It was not until long after his death in 1820 that it was discovered that he was all along a government agent and had been paid enormous sums of secret service money for his work. He got a special payment for keeping them informed of Emmet's private conversations. This loathsome individual encouraged young men to join the United Irishmen, then informed on them and had them arrested and then collected his fees for defending them in court.

On September 15, Emmet was brought to Green Street Courthouse and formally charged with treason. His trial was fixed for Monday, September 19.

CHAPTER 9

R OBERT EMMET was tried before a Special Commission in Green Street Courthouse, on Monday, September 19, 1803. The Presiding Judge was Lord Norbury (John Toler), assisted by Baron George and Baron Daly. The prisoner was brought in chains to the dock and the room was filled with a large crowd of onlookers, the vast majority of them hostile to the defendant. The proceedings began at about 9.30am and lasted all day. A jury of twelve men was empanelled.

The prosecution was led by the Attorney-General, Standish O'Grady, assisted by William Conygnham Plunket and five other counsel. The initial presentation of the case was made by O'Grady, nineteen witnesses were called for the prosecution, none for the defence, and Plunket made the closing argument. In effect, Emmet practically refused to defend himself. He rarely allowed his counsel to cross-examine the witnesses, as most of what they said was true.

The Crown case was based on an old fourteenth century statute from the era of Edward III, accusing the prisoner of encompassing and imagining the death of the King, forming an alliance with the King's enemies and attempting to wage war against the Crown. Others had already been tried by the Special Commission but O'Grady maintained that they were "comparatively speaking, insignificant persons". Emmet, by contrast was "not a person who has been seduced by others, but a gentleman to whom the rebellion may be traced, as the origin, the life and the soul of it". He described the Rising as "unexampled for wanton wickedness in any country, ancient or modern".

Sarah Curran's final letter was quoted in evidence. O'Grady did not reveal her name but said that it seems "to have been written by a brother conspirator acquainted with his schemes and participating in his crimes".

The witnesses included the solicitor who prepared the lease of the Butterfield Lane house to "Robert Ellis" and the man who lived next door, as well as John Fleming, a Republican who had done a deal with the state to avoid prosecution and who now testified about all he had seen at the Marshalsea Lane depot. A number of English officers and soldiers also testified. So also did Joseph Palmer, the owner of the house at Harold's Cross in which Emmet was arrested. He did so reluctantly, to avoid prosecution for harbouring a fugitive. The final witness was Major Sirr.

The Crown had made an overwhelming case in their terms and Emmet forbade his lawyers from making any arguments on his behalf. He had planned and led an Insurrection and he was not going to deny his role in it.

The courtroom was packed and the atmosphere stifling. At one stage a sympathiser passed some sprigs of lavender to Emmet to refresh him. They were instantly snatched from him for fear of poison. Emmet smiled scornfully.

William C Plunket now made a closing statement on behalf of the prosecution. This man had been a close friend of Thomas Addis Emmet since their days together at college and had opposed the Act of Union. He made a brilliant presentation to the court. His speech was a venomous, sarcastic attack on the Rising and on Emmet himself. For this he was later promoted to the position of Solicitor General, but lost the respect of Thomas Addis and of many other people.

Plunket's speech was a tirade of denunciation, delivered with great composure. What angered the Emmets and their extended family and friends was that Plunket would have known Robert Emmet's fine character. But in order to ingratiate himself with the government of the day he attacked the accused's motives and good reputation. He indulged in downright character assassination.

The others, said Plunket were "the illiterate victims of the ambition of this young man", but Emmet was "the centre, the life-blood and the soul of this atrocious conspiracy".

He dismissed Emmet and his fellow Republicans as "a few desperate, obscure, contemptible adventurers in the trade of revolution". He had "stooped from the honourable situation in which his birth, talents and his education had placed him, to debauch the minds of the lower orders of ignorant men with the phantoms of liberty and equality". He had consorted with working-class people, "the bricklayer, the baker, the old clothes man, the hodman and the hostler". He had "let loose the rabble of the country and their crimes were atrocious, wicked and abominable". And of course he accused him of an alliance with the usurper of the French throne against Britain.

Wickham reported Plunket's speech as "most eloquent and most masterly. It was delivered on purpose to show his entire and unqualified denunciation

Marshalsea Lane (Mass Lane), off Thomas Street,
where one of Emmet's arms depots was situated.
This photograph was taken by JJ Reynolds and published in 1903.

of his former principles, his determination, on due and mature reflection, to support the Union, after having been its inveterate opposer, and to stand or fall with the present administration."

When Plunket had finished his address, Lord Norbury spoke to the jury. He concluded by saying: "if you believe the evidence, it is direct proof of all the treasons charged against him. But I say, if you have a doubt, you should acquit him. If you do not, you should find him guilty".

The jury did not even retire to consider their verdict. They stayed in their box, deliberated for a few minutes and then the foreman addressed the court: "My Lord, I have consulted my brother jurors and we are all of the opinion that the prisoner is guilty".

Then the Clerk of the Crown asked Emmet: "What have you therefore now to say, why the judgement of death and execution should not be awarded against you according to law?"

It was now 9.30pm. There had been no break for refreshments. The courtroom was full, of some friends but mostly enemies. The press were there and a few artists who had come to sketch pictures of the prisoner, who was all the time in chains and now tired and hungry. There was a great mass of people in the streets outside, all sympathetic to Emmet and his family, who were held in the highest esteem.

The hour which now followed the clerk's question to the prisoner was probably Robert Emmet's finest hour of his twenty-five years on this earth. If ever a man or woman rose to the demands of an occasion or situation Emmet did now. He was particularly anxious to answer those who had besmirched his character and he wanted to ensure that his motives, which were noble and generous, would not be misunderstood. The lessons in elocution and drama which he received at Samuel Whyte's school stood to him now. His experiences in the cut and thrust of debate in the Trinity College debating societies enabled him to contend with Lord Norbury's interruptions and even turn these intrusions to his advantage.

There is no one authentic authoritative version of Robert Emmet's speech from the dock. William Ridgeway was a crown lawyer and court reporter, but his version is considered somewhat suspect, not just because he was a government official but also because in the days that followed, the Castle authorities published spurious and mendacious accounts of what Emmet had said. In particular, they misrepresented what he said about the French, in order to drive a wedge between the United Irishmen and the French government and to create ill-feeling.

Dr Madden interviewed many people who were present in the court on that day, and while his text cannot be said to be totally correct either, it is the version which has been generally accepted as the more reliable.

Leon Ó Broin has remarked that "Dr Madden submitted all the versions to trustworthy persons so that the report given in his memoirs of Emmet may be taken to contain the substance of the speech and much of the actual language". There is of course substantial agreement between both Madden's and Ridgeway's texts. The version given here is based on Dr Madden's research.

Emmet, despite his chains, his hunger and his fatigue, mustered all his reserves of stamina and eloquence. His voice was loud, strong and clear and he spoke without notes, pen or paper. Dr. Madden says that "he pronounced the speech in so loud a voice as to be distinctly heard at the outer doors of the courthouse... moving about the dock with rapid but not ungraceful motions." He spoke with passion, but also with dignity, clarifying his motives, rebutting the unfounded slanders on his character and finally appealing to the judgement, not of this court and jury, but of posterity, "when other times and other men can do justice to my character".

Chapter 10

⪢◈⪡

Robert Emmet's Speech from the Dock

"I am asked what I have to say why sentence of death should not be pronounced on me, according to law. I have nothing to say that can alter your predetermination, nor that it will become me to say, with any view to the mitigation of that sentence which you are to pronounce and I must abide by. But I have that to say which interests me more than life and which you have laboured to destroy. I have much to say why my reputation should be rescued from the load of false accusation and calumny which has been cast upon it. I do not imagine that, seated where you are, your minds can be so free of prejudice as to receive the least impression from what I am going to utter.

"I have no hope that I can anchor my character in the breast of a court constituted and trammelled as this is. I only wish, and that is the utmost that I can expect, that your lordships may suffer it to float down your memories untainted by the foul breath of prejudice, until it finds some more hospitable harbour to shelter it from the storms by which it is buffeted. Were I only to suffer death, after being adjudged guilty by your tribunal, I should bow in silence and meet the fate that awaits me without a murmur; but the sentence of the law which delivers my body to the executioner will through the ministry of the law, labour in its own vindication, to consign my character to obloquy; for there must be guilt somewhere, whether in the sentence of the court or in the catastrophe, time must determine.

"A man in my situation has not only to encounter the difficulties of fortune, and the force of power over minds which it has corrupted or subjugated, but the difficulties of established prejudice. The man dies, but his memory lives. That mine may not perish, that it may live in the respect of my countrymen, I seize upon this opportunity to vindicate myself from some of the charges alleged against me. When my spirit shall be wafted to a more friendly port, when my shade shall have joined the bands of those martyred heroes who have shed their blood on the scaffold and in the field in defence of their country and of virtue, this is my hope:

"I wish that my memory and my name may animate those who survive me, while I look down with complacency on the destruction of that perfidious government which upholds its domination by blasphemy of the Most High; which displays its power over man as over the beasts of the forest; which sets man upon his brother, and lifts his hand in the Name of God, against the throat of his fellow who believes or doubts a little more or a little less than the government standard, a government which is steeled to barbarity by the cries of the orphans and the tears of the widows it has made."

Here Lord Norbury interrupted Emmet, saying that the mean and wicked enthusiasts who felt as he did, were not equal to the accomplishment of their wild designs.

"The massacres and murders committed in one night by those under your command show them to be barbarians and ruffians, to imbue their hands in the dearest blood of the country in furtherance of your vain boasting that you would take the possession of the Castle of Dublin."

Emmet replied:
"I appeal to the immaculate God, I swear by the Throne of Heaven, before which I must shortly appear, by the blood of the murdered patriots who have gone before me, that my conduct has been, through all this peril, and through all my purposes, governed only by the conviction which I have uttered, and by no other view than that of the emancipation of my country from the super-inhuman oppression under which she has so long and too patiently travailed; and I confidently hope that, wild and chimerical as it may appear, there is still union and strength in Ireland to accomplish this noblest of enterprises.

"Of this I speak with confidence, with intimate knowledge, and with the consolation that appertains to that confidence. Think not, my lords, I say this for the petty gratification of giving you a transitory uneasiness. A man who never yet raised his voice to assert a lie will not hazard his character with posterity by asserting a falsehood on a subject so important to his country, and on an occasion like this. Yes, my lords, a man who does not wish to have his epitaph written until his country is liberated, will not leave a weapon in the power of envy, or a pretence to impeach the probity which he means to preserve, even in the grave to which tyranny consigns him."

Here he was again interrupted by Norbury.

Emmet continued:
"Again I say that what I have spoken was not intended for your lordship, whose situation I commiserate rather than envy – my expressions were for my countrymen. If there is a true Irishman present, let my last words cheer him in the hour of his affliction."

Here he was again interrupted. Lord Norbury said:
"You are making an avowal of dreadful treason, and of a determined purpose to have persevered in them, which I do believe has astonished your audience."

Emmet continued:
"I have always understood it to be the duty of a judge, when a prisoner has been convicted, to pronounce the sentence of the law. I have also understood that judges sometimes think it their duty to hear with patience, and to speak with humanity; to exhort the victim of the laws, and to offer, with tender benignity, their opinions of the motives by which he was adjudged guilty. That a judge has thought it his duty so to have done, I have no doubt; but where is the boasted freedom of your institutions, where is the vaunted impartiality, clemency and mildness of your courts of justice if an unfortunate prisoner, whom your policy and not justice is about to deliver into the hands of the executioner, is not suffered to explain his motives sincerely and truly, and to vindicate the principles by which he was actuated? My lord, it may be a part of the system of angry justice to bow a man's mind by humiliation to the purposed ignominy of the scaffold; but worse to me than the purposed shame or the scaffold's terrors would be the shame of such foul and unfounded imputations as have been laid against me in this court.

"You, my lord, are a judge; I am the supposed culprit. I am a man; you are a man also. By a revolution of power we might exchange places, though we never could change characters. If I stand at the bar of this court and dare not vindicate my character, what a farce is your justice! If I stand at this bar and dare not vindicate my character, how dare you calumniate it? Does the sentence of death which your unhallowed policy inflicts on my body, condemn my tongue to silence and my reputation to reproach?

"Your executioner may abridge the period of my existence; but while I exist I shall not forebear to vindicate my character and motives from your aspersion; and as a man to whom fame is dearer than life, I will make the last use of that life in doing justice to that reputation which is to live after me, and which is the only legacy I can leave to those I honour and love and for whom I am proud to perish. As men, my lords, we must appear on the great day at one common tribunal; and it will then remain for the Searcher of all hearts to show a collective universe, who was engaged in the most virtuous actions or swayed by the purest motives – my country's oppressor or . . ."

Here Norbury interrupted again:
"If you have anything to urge in point of law, you will be heard; but what you have hitherto said, confirms and justifies the verdict of the jury".

Emmet, in reply, continued:
"My lords, will a dying man be denied the legal privilege of exculpating himself in the eyes of the community from an undeserved reproach, thrown upon him during his trial, by charging him with ambition and attempting to cast away for paltry consideration the liberties of his country? Why did your lordships insult me? Or rather, why insult justice, in demanding of me why sentence of death should not be pronounced against me? I know, my lords, that form prescribes that you should ask the question.

"The form also presents the right of answering. This, no doubt, may be dispensed with and so might the whole ceremony of the trial, since sentence was already pronounced at the Castle before the jury was empanelled. Your lordships are but the priests of the oracle, and I insist on the whole of the forms.

"I am charged with being an emissary of France. An emissary of France! And for what end? It is alleged that I wished to sell the independence of my country. And for what end? Was this the object of my ambition? And this is the mode by which a tribunal of justice reconciles contradiction? No, I am no emissary; and my ambition was to hold a place among the deliverers of my country, not in power nor in profit, but in the glory of the achievement. Sell my country's independence to France! And for what? Was it a change of masters? No, but for my ambition. O, my country, was it a personal ambition that could influence me? Had it been the soul of my actions, could I not by my education and fortune, by the rank and consideration of my family, have placed myself amongst the proudest of your oppressors?

"My country was my idol. To it I sacrificed every selfish, every endearing sentiment, and for it I now offer up myself, O God! No, my lords; I acted as an Irishman, determined on delivering my country from the yoke of a foreign and unrelenting tyranny and the more galling yoke of a domestic faction, which is its joint partner and perpetrator in the patricide, from the ignominy existing with an exterior of splendour and a conscious depravity. It was the wish of my heart to extricate my country from this doubly riveted despotism; I wished to place her independence beyond the reach of any power on earth. I wished to exalt her to that proud station in the world. Connection with France was, indeed, intended, but only as far as mutual interest would sanction or require. Were the French to assume any authority inconsistent with the purest independence, it would be the signal for their destruction.

"We sought their aid and we sought it as we had assurance we should obtain it – as auxiliaries in war and allies in peace. Were the French to come as invaders or enemies, uninvited by the wishes of the people, I should oppose them to the utmost of my strength. Yes, my countrymen, I should advise you to meet them upon the beach with a sword in one hand and a torch in the other. I would meet them with all the destructive fury of war. I would animate my countrymen to immolate them in their boats, before they had contaminated the soil of my country. If they succeeded in landing, and if forced to retire before superior discipline, I would dispute every inch of the ground, burn every blade of grass, and the last entrenchment of liberty should be my grave. What I could not do myself, if I should fall, I should leave as a last charge to my countrymen to accomplish; because I should feel conscious that life, any more than death, is unprofitable when a foreign nation holds my country in subjection.

"But it was not as an enemy that the soldiers of France were to land. I looked, indeed, for the assistance of France, but I wished to prove to France and to the world that Irish men deserved to be assisted; that they were indignant at slavery, and ready to assert the independence and liberty of their country. I wished to procure for my country the guarantee which Washington procured for America; to procure an aid which, by its example would be as important as its valour – disciplined, gallant, pregnant with science and experience, that of a people who would perceive the good and polish the rough points of our character. They would come to us as strangers and leave us as friends, after sharing in our perils and elevating our destiny. These were my objects; not to receive new taskmasters, but to expel old tyrants. It was for these ends I sought aid from France; because France, even as an enemy, could not be more implacable than the enemy already in the bosom of my country."

Here he was interrupted by Norbury who shouted his name:
"Mr. Emmet! You have had a most patient trial. We have listened to you with

great patience. It was proved in evidence that by your conduct you excited and encouraged others to join in the insurrection and rebellion. It is an insult to the judges of the land to sit here and listen to expressions of treason. It is an insult to the law which we cannot suffer to be heard in a court of justice. You have been charged with the crime of high treason. That charge has been supported by evidence, and the jury, upon their oaths, have found you guilty. Is there anything in point of law that you can urge in your defence?"

"I have been charged with that importance in the efforts to emancipate my country as to be considered the key-stone of the combination of Irishmen; or as it has been expressed 'the life-blood and soul of the conspiracy'. You do me honour over much; you have given to the subaltern all the credit of the superior. There are men concerned in this conspiracy who are not only superior to me, but even to your own conception of yourself, my lord; men before the splendour of whose genius and virtues I should bow with respectful deference and who would not deign to call you friend, who would not disgrace themselves by shaking your blood-stained hand."

Norbury was stung by this and retorted:
"It is your own hands that are blood-stained. It is you who are responsible for the bloodshed."

Emmet continued:
"What! my lord, shall you tell me, on the passage to the scaffold, which the tyranny (of which you are only the intermediary executioner) has erected for my murder, that I am accountable for all the blood that has been shed and will be shed in this struggle of the oppressed against the oppressor; shall you tell me this, and must I be so very a slave as not to repel it? I do not fear to approach the Omnipotent Judge to answer for the conduct of my whole life; and am I to be appalled and falsified by a mere remnant of mortality here? By you, too, although if it were possible to collect all the innocent blood that you have shed in your unhallowed ministry in one great reservoir, your lordship might swim in it."

Here Norbury interrupted again:
"Instead of showing anything in point of law why judgement should not pass, you have proceeded in a manner the most unbecoming a person in your situation; you have avowed and endeavoured to vindicate principles totally subversive of

the Government – totally subversive of the tranquillity, well-being and happiness of that country which gave you birth – and you have broached treason the most abominable."

Emmet replied:

"Let no man dare, when I am dead, to charge me with dishonour; let no man attaint my memory by believing that I could have engaged in any cause but that of my country's liberty and independence; or that I could have become the pliant minion of power in the oppression of my country. The Proclamation of the Provisional Government speaks for our views; no inference can be tortured from it to countenance barbarity or debasement at home, or subjection, humiliation or treachery from abroad. I would not have submitted to a foreign oppressor, for the same reason that I would resist the foreign and domestic oppressor. In the dignity of freedom I would have fought upon the threshold of my country, and its enemy would enter only by passing over my lifeless corpse. And am I who lived but for my country, and have subjected myself to the dangers of the jealous and watchful oppressor, and the bondage of the grave, only to give my countrymen their rights, and my country her independence, am I to be loaded with calumny and not suffered to resent it? No; God forbid!"

Here Norbury told the prisoner that his sentiments and language disgraced his family and education.

"You sir," he said, "had the honour to be a gentleman by birth, and your father filled a respectable station under the government. You had an eldest brother whom death snatched away, and who when living was one of the greatest ornaments of the bar. The laws of this country were the study of his youth, and the study of his maturer life was to cultivate and support them. He left you a proud example to follow, and if he had lived he would have given your talents the same virtuous direction as his own, and have taught you to admire and preserve that constitution, for the destruction of which you have conspired with the most profligate and abandoned, and associated yourself with hostlers, bakers, butchers, and such persons whom you invited to councils, when you created your provisional government. When you sallied forth at midnight with such a band of assassins, and found yourself implicated in their atrocities, your heart must have lost all recollection of what you were."

This censure angered Emmet, who had learned his idealism from his father, and he replied:

"If the spirit of the illustrious dead participate in the concerns and cares of those who were dear to them in this transitory life, O, ever dear and venerated shade of my departed father, look down with scrutiny upon the conduct of your suffering son, and see if I have, even for a moment, deviated from those principles of morality and patriotism which it was your care to instil into my youthful mind, and for which I am now about to offer up my life!

"My lords, you are impatient for the sacrifice. The blood which you seek is not congealed by the artificial terrors which surround your victim; it circulates warmly and unruffled through the channels which God created for noble purposes, but which you are now bent to destroy, for purposes so grievous that they cry to heaven. Be yet patient! I have but a few more words to say.

"I am going to my cold and silent grave. My lamp of life is nearly extinguished. I have parted with everything that was dear to me in this life for my country's cause and abandoned another idol I adored in my heart, the object of my affections. My race is run. The grave opens to receive me and I sink into its bosom. I have but one request to ask at my departure from this world. It is – the charity of its silence. Let no man write my epitaph; for as no man who knows my motives dares now vindicate them, let not prejudice or ignorance asperse them. Let them and me rest in obscurity and peace; and my tomb remain uninscribed and my memory in oblivion until other times and other men can do justice to my character. When my country takes her place among the nations of the earth, then, and *not till then, let my epitaph be written. I have done.*"

It was with these remarkable, impressive and historic words that Emmet finished his speech from the dock. It was a powerful performance which moved and inspired all who heard it.

Years later, in 1842, St John Mason, Emmet's first cousin, using the pseudonym "Verax", wrote a letter in his defence to *The Times* (London). He said he regarded the Rising "with absolute and unqualified condemnation", but added:

> "Nevertheless, I must say that he was great amid all his errors. When, on the day of his trial – the tomb already open to receive him – he made the very walls ring with the power of his eloquence. I saw that viper (Plunket) whom his father

had nourished in his bosom tremble under his lashes and that scum of humanity (Norbury), who was one of his judges, grow pale and tremble on his seat. It was, under such circumstances, an effort almost superhuman: and when, after inflicting that memorable chastisement, and hurling that withering defiance at his enemies, he defended the principles on which his conduct reposed, he displayed a moral integrity, a talent and intrepidity unparalleled in the annals of the world."

One of Emmet's enemies, the Marquis d'Harcourt, an English officer who had helped to put down the Rising, wrote:

"Never shall I forget the moment when, rising with a manner full of grace and mildness, Emmet offered to his country the sacrifice of his life. All eyes filled with tears. We went out sobbing, and I thought for a moment that justice was severe and the conspirator to be pitied."

It is little wonder then that Emmet's speech from the dock has become one of the greatest in the annals of oratory, and that it has inspired lovers of freedom and justice in Ireland and elsewhere. The great Abraham Lincoln knew this speech and used it as a model. It is said that he learned it by the firelight of his Kentucky cabin.

The attempts by the English authorities to blacken Emmet's name by distorting his last words, selling bogus versions on the streets of Dublin, failed totally. Too many people knew of his fine character, too many had heard the speech and made notes on the day. This ensured that the people of Ireland and the world at large came to know and admire it, and to know and admire the man himself.

THE TRIAL
AND
DYING BEHAVIOUR
OF
Mr R. Emmett,

Who was Executed September the 20th, for High Treafon.—Together with his Solemn Exhortâtion to his Countrymen to rejeét the proffered Friendſhip and Aſſiſtance of Deſpotic, Cruel, and Perfidious FRANCE.

ON Monday September 19, ROBERT EMMETT was put to the bar, at Dublin, on trial for High Treafon. The prifoner challenged nineteen peremptorily out of the pannel for a Petit Jury, and fix were fet afide by the Crown.

The Attorney General took a retrofpective view of the public calamities incident to ,the fpirit of infurrection which had hitherto prevailed the minds of the common people of that country.

The prifoner at the bar, If Mr. Attorney was properly inftruéted, would appear by fubftantial evidence, together with a variety of corroborating circumftances, to have been the prime fource, origin, and fpirit of the recent infurrection in this city fo enormoufly wicked in the conception, but fo truly contempuble and puerile both in the plan and execution.

The prifoner in a fpeech marked by fome traits of ingenuity and elocution. juftified the conduct imputed to him, on firm and long adopted principles.

The Jury returned a verdiét GUILTY, without leaving the box; and Lord Norbury pronounced fentence of DEATH on him.

At ten o'clock this morning, (Sept. 20), a confidential friend of this unfortunate Gentleman was permitted to vifit him at Kilmainham gaol. The vifitor a Profeffional Gentleman of confiderable eminence, on his entrance into the culprit's chamber found him reading the Litany in the fervice of the Church of England in the prefence of the Rev. Mr. Gamble, the Ordinary of Newgate; after which he made a hearty breakfaft. Retiring afterwards to a room with his friend, after certain family communications, he adverted to the circumftance of having his pockets examined in the dock on the preceding evening, for fome inftrument with which it was apprehended he might deftroy himfelf. He difclaimed fuch notion, alledging it was incompatible with the religion he profeffed.

The culprit was led from Kilmainham gaol under a strong military guard, compofed of detachments both of Cavalry and Infantry of the Regular Troops quartered at the Barracks. He arrived about three o'clock at the temporary gallows, in Thomas-ftreet, in a carriage with two clergy-

men. In his progress thither his demeanour, however, did not appear of that ferious caft befitting the awfulnefs of his fituation, or the religious fentiments he had uttered in the morning. He gazed about, particularly in Dirty-lane, the fcene of his exploits, with a fpecies of light inattentive fmile, approaching a laugh, until he was carried to the place of execution, and fpoke and nodded to fome of his acquaintance with the greateft coolnefs. After mounting the platform attached to the gallows, he addreſsed the furr unding crowd in a few words, faying he died in peace and univerfal love and kindnefs with all mankind. While the Executioner was adjufting the rope round his neck, he became very pale, and he feemed earneftly to talk and expoftulate with him moft probably about fome awkwardnefs in his manner, from which he felt an inconvenience. After the hangman had pulled a cap over his eyes, the culprit put up his hands, pinioned as they were, and parily removed it. The platform was dextroufly removed. After which he hung for near a minute quite motionlefs, but violent convulfions then feized him, which lafted for feveral minutes. The process of beheading, &c. was afterwards gone through, and his body removed to Newgate.

The admirable description which he drew of the French fraternity muft powerfully oprate on that part of the people of Ireland, who feek, through the agency of the Firft Conful to difunite thefe countries.

"I have," faid he, "been accufed of being actuated by a wifh to bring about a revolution of this country, through the means of French influence. I deny that either myfelf or the Provifonal Government, had any fueh idea in contemplation. Our own refources were fufficient to accomplifh the object. As to French interpofition, it cannot be too much deprecated: and I exhort the'people of Ireland to beware of fuch affiftance. I urge them in the ftrongeft manner to burn their houfes—nay even the very grafs on which a Frenchman fhall land. Various opportunities have occured to me of witneffing the mifery and defola ion. they have produced in every country where they have gained an entrance, under the fallacious pretences of aiding the Inhabitants who confidered themfelves in a ftate of oppreffion."

Jones & Co, Printers, Upper Mary Area's b.

This bulletin was published by the Dublin Castle authorities on the evening of Robert Emmet's execution and distributed in the city. The intention was to misrepresent what he had said at his trial about French assistance in freeing Ireland from English rule.

54

Chapter 11

———◇———

WHEN EMMET HAD FINISHED SPEAKING, Lord Norbury pronounced the sentence of death and ordered that the execution be carried out the next day, Tuesday, September 20, 1803. A group of young men moved towards the dock, shook the prisoner's hand and bade him farewell. They were Trinity students and they wore the King's uniform. What they did they did instinctively, showing their admiration for an honest and idealistic man. They were called to account afterwards for shaking the hand of a condemned traitor, but they were more honourable than Leonard McNally, the deceiver who leaned over the rail and kissed Emmet on the cheek.

Newgate prison was located next door to the courthouse and the condemned man was brought there. He was later transferred to Kilmainham under heavy escort. He spent most of the night writing letters. One of these was to Richard Curran, brother of Sarah, in which he expressed thanks for his good wishes and regret for the grief he had caused his sister:

> "I intended as much happiness for Sarah as the most ardent love could have given her… it was an attachment increasing every hour, from an admiration of the purity of her mind and respect for her talents. I did dwell in secret upon the prospect of our union… I did not look for honours for myself, praise I would have asked from the lips of no man; but I would have wished to read in the glow of Sarah's countenance that her husband was respected."

Then he spoke directly to her:

> "My love, Sarah! It was not thus that I thought I would have requited your affection. I did hope to be a prop round which your affection might have clung, and which would never have been shaken; but a rude blast has snapped it, and they have fallen over a grave."

His last letter to his brother, Thomas Addis and his wife Jane was as follows:

""My dearest Tom and Jane,

"I am just going to do my last duty to my country. It can be done as well on the scaffold as on the field. Do not give way to any weak feelings on my account, but rather encourage proud ones that I have possessed fortitude and tranquillity of mind to the last.

"God bless you, and the young ones that are growing up about you. May they be more fortunate than their uncle, but may they preserve as pure and ardent an attachment to their country as he has done. Give the watch to little Robert. He will not prize it the less for having been in the possession of two Roberts before him.

"I have one dying request to make to you. I was attached to Sarah Curran, the youngest daughter of your friend. I did hope to have had her for my companion for life. I did hope that she would not only have constituted my happiness, but that her heart and understanding would have made her one of Jane's dearest friends. I know that Jane would have loved her on my account and I feel also that had they been acquainted she must have loved her on her own.

"No one knew of the attachment until now, nor is it now generally known, therefore do not speak of it to others. She is living with her father and brother, but if these protectors should fall off and that no other should replace them, treat her as my wife, and love her as a sister. God Almighty bless and preserve you all. Give my love to all my friends."

He also wrote a detailed account of the Rising and of the preparations made for it. This was an elaborate well-written document in which he listed all the mishaps and reverses, and admitted, "had I another week, had I one thousand pounds, had I one thousand men, I would have feared nothing . . . but there was failure in all, plan, preparation and men."

The double-dealing Dr Edward Trevor promised to deliver all of these communications, but sent them all down to the Castle. Before he died, Thomas Addis read the assessment of the Rising's failure in a book entitled *The Plan of the Insurrection in Dublin and the Causes of its Failure*, written by WH Curran, another son of John Philpot Curran. It had been leaked to him by two civil servants.

The only visitors Emmet had in his last hours were two clergymen, the Rev Gamble and the Rev Grant, and his lawyer, Leonard McNally. The clergymen tried to get him to admit guilt for what he had done. This he stoutly refused to do, but he declared himself to be a Christian and expressed a general repentance for all his sins. He said that what he felt he felt sincerely and would "avow his principles in his last moments". The killing of Lord Kilwarden and his nephew troubled him and he "solemnly declared" that he had left Dublin before this happened. Gamble then prayed with him and "felt himself justified in administering the sacrament". He then added: "The behaviour of Mr Emmet during the solemnity was marked with reverence and propriety."

McNally visited him in the morning and had a long conversation with him. This was of course very much an approved visit, and he made a lengthy report to the Castle afterwards. This report is in the state papers and historians agree it should be treated with the utmost caution. McNally was receiving secret service money. In order to justify his payments and maybe inflate them, he would have exaggerated the importance of this conversation. By the time he had written it Emmet was dead and no one could contradict the author.

McNally had some bad news for Emmet, the news that his mother had died. But he had a strange way of telling him. He asked him if he would like to see his mother. "Oh, what I would not give to see her!" Emmet replied. McNally pointed upwards and said: "Take courage, Robert, you will see her tonight." Thinking that his own circumstances might have hastened her death, Emmet bowed his head and murmured, "it is better so". McNally was truly a wretched scoundrel.

Shortly after one o'clock on the afternoon of Tuesday, September 20, Robert Emmet was taken from his cell in Kilmainham Jail and brought by carriage, under heavy military escort to the place of execution. He was accompanied by the two clergymen. The cortege travelled slowly, crossed the Liffey at Islandbridge, went along the south quays and through Benburb Street, recrossed the river at Queen's Bridge (now Mellows Bridge) and ascended Bridgefoot Street to Thomas Street.

Outside St Catherine's Church a scaffold had been erected. Eight Republican insurgents had recently been hanged on this spot. The scaffold was a makeshift apparatus. A platform had been made by laying planks across barrels. This was almost six feet high and was ascended by a ladder. Two posts rose from the platform to a height of about fifteen feet and a beam was placed across them. From this beam hung a rope with a running noose. Immediately beneath this beam and rope was a narrow plank on which the condemned man would stand.

Emmet maintained a dignity and composure in this awful moment, which his enemies grudgingly acknowledged. The large crowd which had gathered witnessed it. A reporter for *The London Chronicle* admitted: "I never saw a man die like him".

He mounted the scaffold, turned quickly towards the people and said: "My friends, I die in peace, and with sentiments of universal love and kindness to all men." He then shook hands with those on the platform, including Galvin the executioner, to whom he gave whatever money was in his pocket. The rope was placed around his neck and he was blindfolded. Then the executioner kicked the plank from under his feet.

Robert Emmet died bravely, he did not struggle or cry, though he died slowly. The "long drop" had not yet been introduced, and because of his light frame he died slowly and hung on the scaffold for thirty minutes. His body was then taken down and stretched on a deal table on the platform. The hangman cut the head from the body and held it aloft by the hair. He walked up and down the platform and cried out: "Here is the head of the traitor, Robert Emmet."

The body was put in a cheap plain coffin and brought first to Newgate and then to Kilmainham. The artist, James Petrie, made a plaster model for a death mask. Most of Emmet's closest family and friends were in custody and others were afraid to come forward to claim the body in case they too might be arrested. The jailer was ordered to bury the body in Bully's Acre, where paupers and criminals were laid.

Shortly afterwards, the body was taken away secretly and buried elsewhere. Gamble, the clergyman, is said to have had a hand in it, but to this very day nobody has been able to say definitively where it is. Various locations have been mentioned and all of them researched over the last two hundred years. These include St Michan's in Church Street, St Anne's in Dawson Street, St Peter's in Aungier Street, St Paul's in North King Street and the old cemetery in Glasnevin. Dr Madden, historian, George Petrie, antiquarian and son of Petrie who made the death mask, Dr TA Emmet, grand-nephew of the patriot, all tried to establish the whereabouts of the body, but without success. Perhaps, now that DNA analysis is at hand, it may be possible to renew the research with a greater prospect of success.

CHAPTER 12

$=\!\!=\!\!\gg\!\cdot\!\diamond\!\cdot\!\ll\!=$

SARAH CURRAN'S HEART was broken. Because she was known to have been privy to Emmet's plans for a Rising few of her family, friends or acquaintances wished to be associated with her. We cannot be sure if her father banished her or just arranged for her to spend some time with friends in different surroundings.

She found kindness and comfort with the family of Mr Cooper Penrose, an independent-minded Quaker in Cork. In November, 1805 she married Captain Robert Henry Sturgeon. It is said that her heart was always with Emmet but that friends encouraged her to marry this soldier of England. All the accounts indicate that he was kind to her.

Sturgeon brought Sarah with him when he was posted to Sicily, but they had to leave in 1807 when the island was threatened by Napoleon's army. Sarah was already pregnant and in July, 1807 had written to Anne Penrose and asked her to be the child's godmother. It is interesting to note that General Henry Fox's wife had befriended her in Sicily. This was the same General Fox who had been GOC of His Majesty's Forces in Ireland in 1803.

During a storm on the return voyage to England, in December 1807, Sarah gave birth to a son on board ship. She called him John, but unfortunately the child died early in January, 1808. She never got over this tragedy and she died herself at Hythe in Kent, England in May, 1808, at the age of 26. She was buried where she was born, in Newmarket – Áth Trasna, in north Co Cork.

Dr Madden discovered this grave in 1858 and had it marked. Thomas Moore probably gave her a more lasting monument when he wrote *She is Far From the Land*.

This was not the only grave marked by Dr Madden, for he did the same for the valiant Anne Devlin. Her story is one of exceptional courage and valour, right to the end of her days. She was subjected to the most severe punishments; she was bribed, threatened and insulted; she was put into solitary confinement and put on a diet of bread and water. At one stage, her father, mother, three brothers and three sisters were in jail.

In a *Memorial of the State Prisoners of Kilmainham*, presented to the Lord

Lieutenant in July, 1804, the removal of Dr Trevor and others in charge of the jail was demanded. The *Memorial* described the inhuman treatment of the political prisoners and noted: "His treatment of all, but particularly of one unfortunate state prisoner – a female – is shocking to humanity and exceeds belief." The female in question was Anne Devlin.

Dr Madden says of her: "The extraordinary sufferings endured, and the courage and fidelity displayed by this young woman have few parallels."

After two-and-a-half years in prison, Anne Devlin was released, in poor health, but unbroken in spirit. She knew a lot about those involved in the Rising of 1803 but she never told her tormentors one iota. She was utterly faithful to Emmet and his comrades.

Anne was now virtually alone in the world. She told Brother Luke Cullen that shortly after her release a timber merchant in New Street called Edward Kennedy, who had spent some time in prison himself, had given her the sum of ten pounds which he had collected from some generous friends. Later on, she married a man called Campbell and they had two children, a boy and a girl. They were still young when her husband died in 1845 and her life from then on was one of extreme poverty.

Dr Madden, compassionate and kind-hearted as ever, sought her out and found her living in a stable yard in John's Lane, supporting herself by laundry work. He made his own appeal and collected ten pounds for her. But he spent a lot of time abroad and could not keep in contact with her.

When he sought her out again in 1851 he discovered that she had died two days previously, at No 2 Little Elbow Lane, where the present Reginald Street joins the Coombe. She was buried in a pauper's grave in Glasnevin Cemetery.

The *Nation* newspaper of September 27, 1851 reported:

> "Died on Thursday last week, after a long life of want, of hard drudgery and many trials and privations, in a wretched hovel in the Liberties, one of the most heroic and true-hearted women known in Irish history, Anne Devlin, who was Robert Emmet's servant in the house at Butterfield Lane, eight and forty years ago...
>
> "This was the woman who bore to be pricked with Yeomen bayonets, to he half-hanged, to be imprisoned for years in a solitary cell of Kilmainham, to see all her kith and kin prison bound, and her young brother foully done to

death by her side; who resisted bribes, threats, torture and death itself with courage that, never, for a second, faltered, sooner than utter one treacherous word of her master.

"And from a squalid alley off the Coombe, after her long struggles and sufferings, this heroic life has at length flown before the throne of God. This day week they carried her mortal remains in a charity coffin to Glasnevin..."

In his goodness, Dr Madden had her reinterred near the O'Connell Circle and erected a monument over her with this inscription:

To the memory of

ANNE DEVLIN (CAMPBELL)

The faithful servant of Robert Emmet,
who possessed some rare and many noble qualities.

Who lived in obscurity and poverty and so died
on the 18th day of September, 1851, aged 70 years.

May she rest in peace. Amen.

Writing in the *Catholic Bulletin*, August, 1917, Hester Piatt wrote:

"With her £500 (Sirr's bribe) Anne could have settled herself in comfort, married well; found many to excuse her action; besides the friends who are ever ready to rally around the well-to-do. Instead, she held fast by her soul's ideal of loyalty and patriotism, choosing rather torture, suffering and friendless poverty... It is the memory of patriots like Anne Devlin which fills us anew with courage and faith."

Anne Devlin was born at Cronebeg, in the parish of Rathdrum, Co Wicklow.

Her cousin, Michael Dwyer, had avoided arrest in the roundup which followed the Rising. He had managed to keep his guerrilla war going in Wicklow since 1798, holding out in difficult circumstances and in the hope of another French landing. This never came, and as a severe winter set in several members of his immediate family were arrested and held in prison. Eventually, on December 14, 1803, he surrendered on terms (negotiated through a local landlord and MP called William Hume) to the Castle authorities. Dwyer was held in Kilmainham until August 1805. It had been decided to deport him.

Dwyer was put on board the ship *Tellicherry* at Queenstown (Cóbh) and brought to New South Wales in Australia. The voyage lasted 174 days. He was later joined by his wife and five of their seven children. In 1813 he was made a District Constable of police in Sydney and died on August 25, 1825, aged 53 years. His wife, Mary Doyle, died in 1861.

There is a magnificent monument, with a Celtic cross, in Waverley Cemetery, Sydney. The main inscription reads: "In loving memory of all who dared and suffered for Ireland in 1798. Pray for the souls of Michael Dwyer the Wicklow chief and Mary his wife whose remains are interred in this vault. Requiescant in pace." The names of seventy-nine other patriots of the period are inscribed elsewhere on this monument, men and women, Protestants, Catholics and Dissenters, including several clergymen. Also on this monument are the names of the executed 1916 leaders and of the ten men who died on hunger strike in the Long Kesh H-Blocks in 1981.

CHAPTER 13

THE STORY OF ROBERT EMMET is a story of both heroism and tragedy. We can now look back on his short life, and, with the benefit of hindsight, assess his contribution, not just to the cause of Irish freedom but to the universal cause of justice. Any such assessment must, if it is to be worthwhile, be rooted in the circumstances of the time in which he lived.

The United Irish movement represented a coming together of various progressive forces at a period in human history which is now regarded as one of the pivotal epochs in the development of civilisation. The American War of Independence and the French Revolution were concerned with national rights and human rights. The groundwork for these changes was prepared by thinkers and writers who proposed a change in our view of people and their place in the world.

Irish separatism was always a strong force in itself and it continued to assert itself, sometimes at great cost, over the centuries. The leaders of the United Irishmen were people who infused this Irish assertion of identity with the ideas of democracy, republicanism and the rights of man. They thus put the Irish freedom struggle into the mainstream of progressive forces in the world.

These leaders were people of ability and education who could have accepted things as they were under the Crown of England and earned position and a comfortable life for themselves and their families. But their charity, their feeling of fraternity, caused them to search for equality and liberty, and to take practical steps to achieve a free and just Ireland. For most of them their unhappy lot was to die in action, face the executioner on the scaffold or go into exile.

To speak of people like Lord Edward Fitzgerald, Theobald Wolfe Tone, Henry Joy McCracken or Robert Emmet in terms of failure alone is to do them a grave injustice. They set a course for the Irish nation, with their appeal to Protestant, Catholic and Dissenter under the common name of Irishman, which has profoundly affected Irish life for more than two centuries, and which will, we trust, eventually bear abundant fruit.

Emmet's Rising was the last effort of that first generation of Irish Republicans to bring about separation from England. Irish history is littered with "if onlys" and "might have beens" and one could get depressed if one dwelt unduly on them. There is an Arabic proverb which says that man learns little from success but much from failure. Succeeding generations learned a lot from the efforts of the men and women of 1798 and 1803.

It was from the failure in 1798 and the lessons learned from that failure than the Rising of 1803 was planned and executed. We have seen how the open mass organisation, organised in an ascending mode was changed into a more covert, secretive, closely-knit movement with key officers being picked from the top in order to keep out the informers and ensure security. We know that they succeeded in this objective because little or no trace can be found of any treachery within the ranks. Right up to the last moment Emmet held the valuable card of surprise in his hand. We know now that despite the accident in the Patrick Street depot on July 16 he could have waited another week or two to get his resources of men and arms into better shape.

While the new organisation delivered optimum security, not enough attention was given to the possible drawbacks or downsides resulting from such a major reorientation. One of these was what would now be explained in terms of the dynamics of leadership. Many good plans had been made but most of those who were about to be involved had no opportunity to practise their roles. There were certainly no dry runs. The initial operations depended on surprise, precision and speed in order to take advantage of the enemy's lack of preparedness. There was no margin of error for indecision, hesitation or uncertainty. There was certainly no room for indiscipline, but how does an officer keep discipline of an untrained volunteer army if he does not already know his men and they have not experienced his control?

Miles Byrne's account and appraisal of 1803 is of significant importance. He could assess it all afterwards with the benefit of hindsight and of his own professional soldier's judgement. He, and others, considered Emmet's plan to have been an excellent one, but he severely criticised his officers for failure to keep discipline. This second major deficiency, a lack of adequate control, which had undermined the 1798 revolt, showed itself again in 1803. But Emmet was probably too hard on himself when he wrote his own report for Thomas Addis from his prison cell. He blamed no one else, but others had undoubtedly let him down.

It must also be said that too much was thrust on the young Robert Emmet himself. He was a man of talent, even of genius. He had intellectual abilities, as we know from his manifesto and his speech from the dock. His many inventions show that he was also a practical, realistic and sensible man. In addition, he appears by all accounts to have been good in the area of what are now called interpersonal skills; he got on well with people.

How much can we expect from any one individual? The man of many talents cannot have all the talents. And, like all of us, Emmet had his failings.

The records, the memoirs, the state papers have all been researched and evaluated over the past two hundred years, and anything that is useful has probably been unearthed by now. There are gaps in our knowledge and one of them is that we do not know what structure there was at the top of the movement at the time. Who was making the decisions? Was there a collective leadership? A collective unified command brings different viewpoints and experience to bear on issues, problems and plans. Was Emmet himself left to make all the decisions? Was too much responsibility thrust upon him? Was he his own director of operations? If so, then it was extraordinary how much he did achieve. Because, but for a few unfortunate mishaps, he almost carried off a spectacular *coup d'état*. After all, Portugal won her freedom from Spain in 1640 with forty men.

Emmet's endowments were considerable, but historians and commentators have drawn attention to his too trusting ways with people. It is possible that he was too ready to take others at their word and inevitably some people let him down. Eager, passionate people can sometimes assume that others are as devoted as they themselves and they can lose touch with reality, the reality of human nature. The enthusiastic Emmet, full of plans and ideas for the Ireland he loved, must have lacked the shrewdness and insight that come from the experience of life. There is a wisdom that comes with the maturity of age; and he was only twenty-five years old. Who are we to find fault with him, if his only serious failing was his lack of years?

William Butler Yeats, with the discerning insight of the poet into people and their ways, has given us this appraisal of young Emmet:

> "He was a very young man. He had not that distrust of human nature which is the bitterest part of wisdom and only comes to men by long experience. He trusted too easily. Men failed him through weakness, through idleness, through all kinds of little, petty weaknesses. Some, too, perhaps were treacherous. His mind was in a flame with

his own thoughts, with his own purposes. But such men , though they see often less into human nature than others until the world has schooled them, have often been the very masters of the world."

We can surmise that Thomas Russell might have been a more successful Commander in Chief, but such speculation would be a useless exercise now. Russell had been in prison from 1796 to 1802 and was a competent soldier and organiser. When he tried to reorganise Antrim and Down in 1803 he found that in the seven years that had elapsed since he was last among the Ulster people a lot had changed.

After the defeat in 1798 some of the Presbyterians vowed that they would never again take on the army of the Crown armed only with pikes; they wanted muskets and they wanted French aid. In addition, they had been fed a potent measure of propaganda which portrayed the Rising in Wexford and Wicklow as being tainted with Catholic sectarianism. Moves were clearly afoot to wean them from the Republican Cause, but had the French come and brought them muskets they would probably have rallied again.

The Anglican Church or Church of Ireland was the established church and possessed great wealth. They occupied extensive estates of land and benefited from tithes collected from the whole population. Emmet's Proclamation proposed to abolish the tithes and take over the church lands and make them the property of the nation. This was the church to which he himself belonged.

Since 1672 the Presbyterian clergy had been provided with money by the State, called the *regium donum* or royal gift. This was really a paltry sum. In 1792 it amounted in total to £5,000. In 1803 the *regium donum* was quintupled. Lord Castlereagh's "plan for strengthening the connection between the Government and the Presbyterian Synod of Ulster" was adopted in 1803. The *donum* was now paid directly to each minister through a government agent who controlled the fund and sat in the Synod. Every effort was being made to detach the Presbyterians or Dissenters from "French principles", while the Orange Order societies were supported. This was the old stratagem of divide and conquer, ruthlessly pursued so as to frustrate the cause of the common name of Irishman.

Irish Republicanism first flourished among the Presbyterians of Ulster and Belfast in particular. They found common cause with their Catholic neighbours and were joined by equally idealistic members of the established church. Belfast became known as "the Athens of the North" during the 1790s because of the lively debates and discussion about all the new ideas. Athens was "the cradle of democracy" and Belfast could have become another cradle of democracy. Instead of that, the generous human ideals of the United Irishmen were suppressed and silenced and the flames of sectarianism were fanned, until the "Athens of the North" became a cauldron of bigotry. Such are the methods of imperialists. Nevertheless, true, generous Republicanism was never totally extinguished among the Protestants and Dissenters of Ulster.

While Emmet's speech from the dock is appreciated for its power, its eloquence and its courage, his proclamation or manifesto is probably equally important. Later Republicans found inspiration in it and one can find echoes of it in the 1916 Proclamation of the Republic and even in the Democratic Programme of the first Dáil Éireann.

Long before the Geneva Conventions on the conduct of war and the treatment of prisoners of war, Robert Emmet had, in his manifesto and the thirty decrees which followed it, laid down some basic elements of a moral framework for these unfortunate, but sometimes necessary, events in human life.

There is much for which we should remember him and be grateful to him. His legacy is considerable. It is appropriate to conclude by quoting the last paragraph of his manifesto:

The Provisional Government strictly exhort and enjoin all magistrates, officers, civil and military, and the whole of the nation, to cause the law of morality to be enforced and respected, and to execute, as far as in them lies, justice with mercy, by which liberty alone can be established, and the blessings of Divine Providence secured.

APPENDICES

Manifesto of the Provisional Government

The Provisional Government to the People of Ireland.

You are now called upon to show the world that you are competent to take your place among nations; that you have a right to claim their recognizance of you, as an independent country; by the only satisfactory proof you can furnish of your capability of maintaining your independence, your wresting it from England with your own hands.

In the development of this system, which has been organized within the last eight months at the close of internal defeat, and without the hope of foreign assistance, which has been conducted with a tranquillity mistaken for obedience, which neither the failure of a similar attempt in England has retarded, nor the renewal of hostilities has accelerated; in the development of this system you will show the people of England, that there is a spirit of perseverance in this country beyond their power to calculate or repress; you will show to them that as long as they think to hold unjust dominion over Ireland, under no change of circumstances can they count on its obedience, under no aspect of affairs can they judge of its intentions; you will show to them that the question which it now behoves them to take into serious consideration, is not whether they will resist a separation, which it is our fixed determination to effect, but whether or not they will drive us beyond separation, whether they will by a sanguinary resistance create a deadly national antipathy between the two countries, or whether they take the only means still left of driving such a sentiment from our minds, by a prompt, manly, and sagacious acquiescence in our just and reasonable determination. If the secrecy with which the present effort has been conducted shall have led our enemies to suppose that its extent must have been partial, a few days will undeceive them. That confidence which was once lost by trusting to external support, and suffering our own means to be gradually undermined, has been again restored. We have been mutually pledged to each other to look only to our own strength, and that the first introduction of a system of terror, the first attempt to execute an individual in one county, should be the signal of insurrection in all. We have now, without the loss of a man, with our means of communication untouched, brought our plans to the moment when they are ripe for execution, and, in the promptitude with which nineteen counties will come forward at once to execute them, it will be found that neither confidence nor communication are wanting to the people of Ireland.

In calling on our countrymen to come forward, we feel ourselves bound, at the same time, to justify our claim to their confidence by a precise declaration of our views. We therefore solemnly declare that our object is to establish a free and independent Republic in Ireland; that the pursuit of this object we will relinquish only with our lives; that we will never, unless at the express call of our country, abandon our posts until the acknowledgement of its independence is obtained from England, and that we will enter into no negotiations (but for exchange of prisoners) with the government of that country while a British army remains in Ireland. Such is the declaration on which we call first on that part of Ireland which was once paralysed by the want of intelligence, to show that to that cause only was its inaction to be attributed; on that part of Ireland which was once foremost in its fortitude in suffering; on that part of Ireland which once offered to take the salvation of the country on itself; on that part of Ireland where the flame of liberty first glowed; we call upon the North to stand up and shake off their slumber and their oppression.

Men of Leinster! Stand to your arms; to the courage which you have already displayed is your country indebted for the confidence which truth feels in its own strength, and for the dismay with which our enemies will be overcome, when they find this effort to be universal. But, men of Leinster, you owe more to your country than the having animated it by your past example, you owe more to your own courage than the having obtained protection by it. If six years ago you rose without arms, without plan, without co-operation, with more troops against you alone than are now in the country at large, you were able to remain six weeks in open defiance of the government, and within a few miles of the capital, what will you now effect, with that capital, and every other part of Ireland, ready to support you? But it is not on this head we have need to address you. No! we now speak to you, and through you to the rest of Ireland, on a subject dear to us, even as the success of our country – its honour. You are accused by your enemies of having violated that honour by excesses, which they themselves had in their fullest extent provoked, but which they have grossly exaggerated, and which have been attributed to you. The opportunity for vindicating yourselves by action is now for the first time in your power, and we call upon you to give the lie to such assertions, by carefully avoiding all appearance of intoxication, plunder, or revenge, recollecting that you lost Ireland before, not from want of courage, but from not having that courage rightly directed by discipline.

But we trust that your past sufferings have taught you experience, and that you will respect the declaration we now make, which we are determined by every means in our power to enforce. The nation alone has the right, and alone possesses the power of punishing individuals, and whosoever shall put another to death, except in battle, without a fair trial by his country, is guilty of murder. The intention of the Provisional Government of Ireland, is to claim from the English government such Irishmen as have been sold or transported by it for their attachment to freedom; and for this purpose it will retain as hostages, for their safe return, such adherents of that government as shall fall into their hands. It therefore calls upon the people to respect such hostages, and to recollect that in spilling their blood, they would leave their own countrymen in the hands of their enemies.

The intentions of the Provisional Government is to resign its functions as soon as the nation shall have chosen its delegates, but, in the meantime, it is determined to enforce the regulations hereunto subjoined; it, in consequence, takes the property of the country under its protection, and will punish with the utmost rigour any person who shall violate that property, and thereby injure the resources and future prosperity of Ireland.

Whosoever refuses to march to any part of the country he is ordered, is guilty of disobedience to the government, which alone is competent to decide in which place his service is necessary, and which desires him to recollect that in whatever part of Ireland he is fighting, he is still fighting for its freedom. Whoever presumes, by acts or otherwise, to give countenance to the calumny propagated by our enemies that this is a religious contest is guilty of the grievous crime, that of belying the motives of the country. Religious disqualifications are but one of the many grievances of which Ireland has to complain. Our intention is to remove not that only, but every other oppression under which we labour. We fight that all of us may have our country, and, that done, each of us shall have our religion.

We are aware of the apprehensions which you have expressed, that, in quitting your own counties, you leave your wives and children in the hands of your enemies, but on this head have no uneasiness; if there are still men base enough to persecute those who are unable to resist, show them by your victories that you have the power to punish, and, by your obedience, that you have the power to protect, and we pledge ourselves to you that these men shall be made to feel that the safety of every thing they hold dear depends on the conduct they observe to you. Go forth then with confidence, conquer the foreign enemies of your country, and leave to us the care of preserving its internal tranquillity; recollect that not only the victory but also the honour of your country is placed in your hands. Give up your private resentments, and show to the world that the Irish are not only a brave, but also a generous and forgiving people.

Men of Munster and Connaught, you have your instructions, you will execute them. The example of the rest of your countrymen is now before you, your own strength is unbroken; five months ago you were eager to act without any other assistance; we now call upon you to show what you then declared you only wanted, the opportunity of proving that you possess the same love of liberty and the same courage with which the rest of your countrymen are animated.

We turn now to that portion of our countrymen whose prejudices we had rather overcome by a frank declaration of our intentions, than conquer in the field; and, in making this declaration, we do not wish to dwell on events, which, however they may bring ten-fold odium on their authors, must still tend to keep alive in the minds, both of the instruments and victims of them, a spirit of animosity, which it is our wish to destroy. We will enter into no detail of the atrocities and oppressions which Ireland has laboured under, during its connection with England; but we justify our determination to separate from that country, on the broad historical statement, that, during six hundred years, she has been unable to conciliate the affections of the people of Ireland; that, during that time, five rebellions were entered into to shake off the yoke; that she has been obliged to enter into a system of unprecedented torture in her defence; that she has broken every tie of voluntary connection, by taking even the name of independence from Ireland, through the intervention of a parliament notoriously bribed, and not representing the will of the people; that in vindication of this measure, she has herself given the justification of the views of the United Irishmen, by declaring in the words of her ministers, 'That Ireland never had, and never could enjoy, under the then circumstances, the benefits of British connection; that it necessarily must happen, when one country is connected with another, that the interests of the lesser will be borne down by the greater. That England had supported, and encouraged the English colonist in their oppression towards the natives of Ireland; that Ireland had been left in a state of ignorance, rudeness, and barbarism, worse in its effects, and more degrading in its nature, than that in which it was found six centuries before.' (This is a quotation from Lord Castlereagh's speech.) Now to what cause are these things to be attributed? Did the curse of the Almighty keep alive a spirit of obstinacy in the minds of the Irish people for six hundred years? Did the doctrines of the French revolution produce five rebellions? Could the misrepresentations of ambitious designing men drive from the mind of a whole people the recollection of defeat, and raise the infant from the cradle, with the same feelings with which its father sank to the grave? Will this gross avowal, which our enemies have made of their own views, remove none of the calumny that has been thrown upon ours? Will none of the credit which has been lavished on them, be transferred to the solemn declaration which we now make in the face of God and our country?

We war not against property, – we war against no religious sect, – we war not against past opinions or prejudices, – we war against English dominion. We will not, however, deny that there are some men, who, not because they have supported the government of our oppressors, but because they have violated the common laws of morality, which exist alike under all, or under no government, have put it beyond our power to give to them the protection of a government. We will not hazard the influence we may have with the people, and the power it may give us of preventing the excesses of revolution, by undertaking to place in tranquillity the man who has been guilty of torture, free-quarter, rape, and murder, by the side of the sufferer or their relations; but in the frankness with which we warn those men of their danger, let those who do not feel that they have passed this boundary of mediation count on their safety.

We had hoped, for the sake of our enemies, to have taken them by surprise, and to have committed the cause of our country before they could have time to commit themselves against it; but, though we have not altogether been able to succeed, we are yet rejoiced to find that they have not come forward with promptitude on the side of those who have deceived them; and we now call upon them, before it is yet too late, not to commit themselves against a people which they are unable to resist, and in support of a government, which, by their own declaration, had forfeited its claim to their allegiance. To that government, in whose hands, though not the issue, at least the features with which the present contest is marked, or placed, we now turn. How is it to be decided? Is open and honourable force alone to be resorted to? Or is it your intention to employ those laws which custom has placed in your hands, and to force us to employ the law of retaliation in our defence?

Of the inefficacy of a system of terror in preventing the people of Ireland from coming forward to assert their freedom, you have already had experience. Of the effect which such a system will have on our minds, in case of success, we have already forewarned you. We now address to you another consideration: if in the question which is now to receive a solemn and we trust final decision; if we have been deceived, reflection would point out that conduct should be resorted to which was the best calculated to produce conviction on our minds.

What would that conduct be?

It would be to show us that the difference of strength between the two countries is such as to render it unnecessary for you to bring out all your forces; to show that you have something in reserve to crush hereafter, not only a greater exertion of the people, but one rendered still greater by foreign assistance. It would be to show us, that what we vainly supposed to be a prosperity growing beyond your grasp, is only a partial exuberance, requiring but the pressure of your hand to reduce to form.

But for your own sakes, do not resort to a system which, while it increases the acrimony of our minds, would leave us under the melancholy delusion, that we had been forced to yield, not to the sound and temperate exertions of your superior strength, but to the frantic struggles of weakness, concealing itself under desperation. Consider that the distinction of rebel and enemy, is of a very fluctuating nature; that during the course of your own experience, you have already been obliged to lay it aside: that should you be obliged to abandon it towards Ireland, you cannot hope to do so as tranquilly as you have done towards America: for in the exasperated state to which you have roused the minds of the Irish people – a people whom you profess to have left in a state of barbarism and ignorance, with what confidence can you say to that people, 'While the advantage of cruelty lay upon our side, we slaughtered you without mercy, but the measure of your own blood is beginning to preponderate. It is no longer our interest that this bloody system should continue, show us then that forbearance which we never taught you by precept or example, lay aside your resentment; give quarter to us, and let us mutually forget we never gave quarter to you.' Cease then, we entreat you, uselessly to violate humanity, by resorting to a system inefficacious as a mode of defence; inefficacious as a mode of conviction; ruinous to the future relations of the two countries in case of our success; and destructive of those instruments of defence which you will then find it doubly necessary to have preserved unimpaired. But if your determination be otherwise, hear ours. We will not imitate you in cruelty; we will put no man to death in cold blood; the prisoners which first fall into our hands shall be treated with the respect due to the unfortunate, but if the life of a single unfortunate Irish soldier is taken after the battle is over, the orders thenceforth to be delivered to the Irish army is, neither to give nor to take quarter. Countrymen, if a cruel necessity force us to retaliate, we will bury our resentment in the field of battle; if we fail, we will fall where we fight for our country. Fully impressed with this determination, of the necessity of adhering to which past experience has but too fatally convinced us; fully impressed with the justice of our cause, which we now put to issue, we make our last and solemn appeal to the sword, and to heaven; and, as the cause of Ireland deserves to prosper, may God give us the victory.

Conformably to the above Proclamation, the Provisional Government of Ireland decree that as follows:

1. From the date and the promulgation hereof, tithes are hereby abolished, and church lands are the property of the nation.
2. From the same date, all transfers of landed property are prohibited, each person paying his rent until the National Government is established; the national will declared, and the courts of justice be organised.
3. From the same date, all transfer of bonds, debentures, and all public securities, are in like manner forbidden, and declared void for the same time, and for the same reason.
4. The Irish Generals, commanding districts, shall seize such of the partisans of England as may serve as hostages, and shall apprise the English Commanders, opposed to them, that a strict retaliation shall take place, if any outrages contrary to the laws of war shall be committed by the troops under command of each; or by the partisans of England in the district which he occupies.
5. That the Irish Generals are to treat, (except where retaliation makes it necessary), the English troops who may fall into their hands, or such Irish as serve in the regular forces of England, and who shall have acted conformably to the laws of war, shall be treated as prisoners of war; but all Irish Militia, Yeomen, or Volunteer Corps, or bodies of Irish, or individuals, who fourteen days after the promulgation and date hereof shall be found in arms, shall be considered as rebels, committed for trial, and their properties confiscated.
6. The Generals are to assemble court-martials, who are to be sworn to administer justice: who are not to condemn without sufficient evidence, and before whom all military offenders are to be sent instantly for trial.
7. No man is to suffer death by their sentence but for mutiny; the sentences of such others as are judged worthy of death, shall not be put into execution until the Provisional Government declares its will; nor are

court-martials on any pretence to sentence, nor is any officer to suffer the punishment of flogging, or any species of torture to be inflicted.

8. The Generals are to enforce the strictest discipline, and to send offenders immediately to the court-martial; and are enjoined to chase away from the Irish armies, all such as shall disgrace themselves by being drunk in the presence of the enemy.

9. The Generals are to apprise their respective armies that all military stores and ammunition, belonging to the English government, be the property of the captors, and the value equally divided, without respect of rank, between them, except that the widows, orphans, parents, or other heirs of those who gloriously fall in the attack, shall be entitled to a double share.

10. As the English nation has made war on Ireland, all English property in ships or otherwise, is subject to the same rule, and all transfer of them forbidden, and declared void in like manner as is expressed in Nos 2, and 3.

11. The Generals of the different districts are hereby empowered to confer rank up to colonels inclusive, on such as they conceive merit it from the nation, but are not to make more colonels than one for fifteen hundred men, nor more lieutenant colonels than one for every thousand men.

12. The Generals shall seize on all sums of public money in the custom houses, in their districts, or in the hands of the different collectors, county treasurers, or other revenue officers, whom they shall render responsible for the sums in their hands. The Generals shall pass receipts for the amount, and account to the Provisional Government for the same.

13. When the people elect their officers up to the colonels, the General is bound to confirm it, no officer can be broke but by sentence of a court-martial.

14. The Generals shall correspond with the Provisional Government, to whom they shall give details of all their operations; they are to correspond with the neighbouring Generals, to whom they are to transmit all necessary intelligence and to co-operate with them.

15. The General commanding in each county shall as soon as it is cleared of the enemy, assemble the County Committee, who shall be elected conformably to the constitution of the United Irishmen. All the requisitions necessary for the army shall be made in writing, by the Generals to the Committee, who are hereby empowered, and enjoined,

to pass receipts for each article to the owners, to the end that they may receive their full value from the nation.

16. The County Committee is charged with the civil direction of the county, the care of the national property, and the preservation of order and justice in the county, for which purpose the County Committee are to appoint a high sheriff, and one or more sub-sheriffs, to execute their orders; a sufficient number of Justices of the Peace for the county; a high, and a sufficient number of petty constables in each barony, who are respectively charged with the duties now performed by those magistrates.

17. The county of Cork, on account of its extent, is to be divided, conformably to the boundaries for raising militia, into the counties of North and South Cork; for each of which a county constable, high sheriff, and all magistrates above directed are to be appointed.

18. The County Committee are hereby empowered and enjoined to issue warrants to apprehend such persons as it shall appear, on sufficient evidence, perpetrated murder, torture, and other breaches of the acknowledged articles of war and morality on the people, to the end that they may be tried for these offences so soon as the competent courts of justice are established by the nation.

19. The County Committee shall cause the sheriff, or his officers, to seize on all the personal property of such, to put seals on their effects, to appoint proper persons to preserve all such property until the national courts of justice shall have decided on the fate of the proprietors.

20. The County Committee shall act in like manner with all state and church lands, parochial estates, and all public lands and edifices.

21. The County Committee shall, in the interim, receive all the rents and debts of such persons, and estates, and give receipts for the same; shall transmit to the Government an exact account of their value, extent, and amount, and receive the directions of the Provisional Government thereon.

22. They shall appoint some proper house in the counties where the sheriff is permanently to reside, and where the County Committee shall assemble; they shall cause all the records and papers of the county to be there transmitted, arranged, and kept, and the orders of the Government to be there transmitted and received.

23. The County Committee is hereby empowered to pay out of these effects, or by assessment, reasonable salaries for themselves, the sheriffs, justices, and other magistrates, whom they shall appoint.

24. They shall keep a written journal of all their proceedings, signed each day by members of the committee, or a sufficient number of them, for the inspection of Government.
25. The County Committee shall correspond with Government on all subjects with which they are charged, and transmit to the General of the district such information as they shall conceive useful to the public.
26. The County Committee shall take care that all State prisoners, however great their offences, shall be treated with humanity, and allow them sufficient support, to the end that the world may know that the Irish nation is not actuated by a spirit of revenge, but of justice.
27. The Provisional Government wishing to commit, as soon as possible, the sovereign authority to the people, direct that each county and city shall elect, agreeably to the constitution of United Irishmen, representatives to meet in Dublin, to whom, the moment they assemble, the Provisional Government will resign its functions, and, without presuming to dictate to the people, they beg leave to suggest, that for the important purpose to which these electors are called, integrity of character should be the first object.
28. The number of representatives being arbitrary, the provisional government have adopted that of the late House of Commons, 300, and according to the best returns of the population of the cities and counties, the following number are to be returned from each: Antrim, 13, Armagh, 9; Belfast Town, 1; Carlow, 3; Cavan, 7; Clare, 8, Cork County, north, 14, Cork County, south, 14; Cork city, 6; Donegal, 10; Down, 16; Drogheda, 1; Dublin county, 4; Dublin city, 14; Fermanagh, 5; Galway, 10; Kerry, 9; Kildare, 14; Kilkenny, 7; King's County, 6; Leitrim, 5; Limerick county, 10; Limerick city, 3; Londonderry, 9; Longford, 4; Louth, 4; Mayo, 12; Meath, 9; Monaghan, 9; Queen's county, 6; Roscommon, 8; Sligo, 6; Tipperary, 13; Tyrone, 14; Waterford county, 6, Waterford city, 2; Westmeath, 5; Wicklow, 5.
29. In the cities the same regulations as in the counties shall be adopted; the city committees shall appoint one or more sheriffs, as they think proper, and shall take possession of all the public and corporation properties in their jurisdiction, in like manner as is directed in counties.
30. The Provisional Government strictly exhort and enjoin all magistrates, officers, civil and military, and the whole of the nation, to cause the law of morality to be enforced and respected, and to execute, as far as in them lies, justice with mercy, by which liberty alone can be established, and the blessings of Divine Providence secured.

Roll of Honour, 1803

Edward Kearney, hanged in Thomas Street, Dublin, September 1.

Owen Kirwan, hanged in Thomas Street, Dublin, September 1.

Maxwell Roach, hanged in Thomas Street, Dublin, September 2.

Denis Lambert Redmond, hanged at Coal Quay (now Wood Quay), Dublin, September 8.

John Killeen, hanged in Thomas Street, Dublin, September 10.

John McCann, hanged in Thomas Street, Dublin, September 10.

Felix Rourke, hanged outside his own home, Rathcoole, September 10.

Thomas Keenan, hanged in Thomas Street, Dublin, September 11.

John Hayes, hanged in Thomas Street, Dublin, September 17.

Michael Kelly, hanged in Thomas Street, Dublin, September 17.

James Byrne, hanged in Townsend Street, Dublin, September 17.

John Begg, hanged in Townsend Street, Dublin, September 17.

Thomas Donnelly, hanged at Palmerstown, Dublin, September 17.

Nicholas Tyrrell, hanged at Palmerstown, Dublin, September 17.

Robert Emmet, hanged in Thomas Street, Dublin, September 20

Henry Howley, hanged at Kilmainham Jail, Dublin, September 28.

John McIntosh, hanged in Patrick Street, Dublin, October 3.

Thomas Russell, hanged at Downpatrick, Co Down, October 21.

James Corry, hanged at Downpatrick, Co Down, October 22.

James Drake, hanged at Downpatrick, Co Down, October 22.

Andrew Hunter, hanged at Carrickfergus, Co Antrim, October 26.

David Porter, hanged at Carrickfergus, Co Antrim, October 26.

Tradesmen were prominent in Robert Emmet's movement in Dublin. Edward Kearney, John Killeen, Thomas Keenan, John Hayes, Michael Kelly, Henry Howley and John McIntosh were carpenters; Owen Kirwan and John Begg were tailors; Thomas Donnelly and Nicholas Tyrrell were factory workers; Maxwell Roach was a slater; Denis Lambert Redmond was a coal factor; John McCann was a shoemaker; Felix Rourke was a farm labourer and James Byrne was a baker.

Robert Emmet and the Ireland of today (1)

*An Address delivered by Patrick H. Pearse at the Emmet Commemoration
in the Academy of Music, Brooklyn, New York, March 2, 1914.*

You ask me to speak of the Ireland of today. What can I tell you of it that is worthy of commemoration where we commemorate heroic faith and the splendour of death? In that Ireland whose spokesmen have, in return for the promise of a poor simulacrum of liberty, pledged to our ancient enemy our loyalty and the loyalty of our children, is there, even though that pledge has been spoken, any group of true men, any right striving, any hope still cherished in virtue of which, lifting up our hearts, we can cry across the years to him whom we remember tonight. "Brother, we have kept the faith; comrade, we, too, stand ready to serve"?

For patriotism is at once a faith and a service. A faith which in some of us has been in our flesh and bone since we were moulded in our mothers' wombs, and which in others of us has at some definite moment of our later lives been kindled flaming as if by the miraculous word of God; a faith which is of the same nature as religious faith and is one of the eternal witnesses in the heart of man to the truth that we are of divine kindred; a faith which, like religious faith, when true and vital, is wonder-working, but, like religious faith, is dead without good works even as the body without the spirit. So that patriotism needs service as the condition of its authenticity, and it is not sufficient to say "I believe" unless one can say also "I serve".

And our patriotism is measured, not by the formula in which we declare it, but by the service which we render. We owe to our country all fealty and she asks always for our service; and there are times when she asks always for our service; and there are times when she asks of us not ordinary but some supreme service. There are in every generation those who shrink from the ultimate sacrifice, but there are in every generation those who make it with joy and laughter, and these are the salt of the generations, the heroes who stand midway between God and men. Patriotism is in large part a memory of heroic dead men and a striving to accomplish some task left unfinished by them. Had they not gone before, made their attempts and suffered the sorrow of their failures, we should long ago have lost the tradition of faith and service, having no memory in the heart nor any unaccomplished dream.

The generation that is now growing old in Ireland had almost forgotten our heroes. We had learned the great art of parleying with our enemy and achieving nationhood by negotiation. The heroes had trodden hard and bloody ways: we should tread soft and flowering ways. The heroes had given up all things; we had learned a way of gaining all things, land and good living and the friendship of our foe. But the soil of Ireland, yea, the very stones of our cities have cried out against an infidelity that would barter an old tradition of nationhood even for a thing so precious as peace. This the heroes have done for us; for their spirits indwell in the place where they lived, and the hills of Ireland must be rent and her cities levelled with the ground and all her children driven out upon the seas of the world before those voices are silenced that bid us to be faithful still and to make no peace with England until Ireland is ours.

I live in a place that is very full of heroic memories. In the room in which I work at St. Enda's College, Robert Emmet is said often to have sat; in our garden is a vine which they call Emmet's Vine and from which he is said to have plucked grapes; through our wood runs a path which is called Emmet's Walk – they say that he and Sarah Curran walked there; at an angle of our boundary wall there is a little fortified lodge called Emmet's Fort. Across the road from us is a thatched cottage whose tenant in 1803 was in Green Street Courthouse all the long day that Emmet stood on trial, with a horse saddled without that he might bring news of the end to Sarah Curran. Half a mile from us across the fields is Butterfield House, where Emmet lived during the days preceding the rising. It is easy to imagine his figure coming out along the Harold's Cross Road to Rathfarnham, tapping the ground with his cane, as they say was his habit; a young, slight figure, with how noble a head bent a little upon the breast, with how high a heroism sleeping underneath that quietness and gravity! One thinks of his anxious nights in Butterfield House; of his busy days in Marshalsea Lane or Patrick Street; of his careful plans – the best plans that have yet been made for the capture of Dublin; his inventions and devices, the jointed pikes, the rockets and explosives upon which he counted so much; his ceaseless conferences, his troubles with his associates, his disappointments, his disillusionments, borne with such sweetness and serenity of temper, such a trust in human nature, such a trust in Ireland! Then the hurried rising, the sally into the streets, the failure at the Castle gates, the catastrophe in Thomas Street, the retreat along the familiar Harold's Cross Road to Rathfarnham. At Butterfield House Anne Devlin, the faithful, keeps watch. You remember her greeting to Emmet in the first pain of her disappointment: "Musha, bad welcome to you! Is Ireland lost by you, cowards that you are, to lead the people to destruction and then to leave them?" And poor Emmet's reply – no word of blame for the traitors that had sold him, for the cravens that had abandoned him, for the fools that had bungled; just a halting, heartbroken exculpation, the only one he was to make for himself – "Don't blame me, Anne; the fault is not mine". And her woman's heart went out to him and she took him in and cherished him; but the soldiery were on his track, and that was his last night in Butterfield House. The bracken was his bed thenceforth, or a precarious pillow in his old quarters at Harold's Cross, until he lay down in Kilmainham to await the summons of the executioner.

No failure, judged as the world judges these things, was ever more complete, more pathetic than Emmet's. And yet he has left us a prouder memory than the memory of Brian victorious at Clontarf or of Owen Roe victorious at Benburb. It is the memory of a sacrifice Christ-like in its perfection. Dowered with all things splendid and sweet, he left all things and elected to die. Face to face with England in the dock at Green Street he uttered the most memorable words ever uttered by an Irishman; words which, ringing clear above a century's tumults, forbid us ever to waver or grow weary until our country takes her place among the nations of the earth. And his death was august. In the great space of Thomas Street an immense silent crowd; in front of St. Catherine's Church a gallows upon a platform, a young man climbs to it, quiet, serene, almost smiling, they say – ah, he was very brave; there is no cheer from the crowd, no groan; this man is to die for them, but no man dares to say aloud "God bless you, Robert Emmet". Dublin must one day wash out in blood the shameful memory of that quiescence. Would Michael Dwyer come from the Wicklow Hills? Up to the last moment Emmet seems to have expected him. He was saying "Not yet" when the hangman kicked aside the plank and his body was launched into the air. They say it swung for half an hour with terrible contortions, before he died. When he was dead the comely head was severed from the body. A friend of mine knew an old woman who told him how the blood flowed down upon the pavement, and how she sickened with horror as she saw the dogs of the street lap up that noble blood. Then the hangman showed the pale head to the people and announced: "This is the head of a traitor, Robert Emmet". A traitor? No, but a true man. O my brothers, this was one of the bravest spirits that Ireland has ever nurtured. This man was faithful even unto the ignominy of the gallows, dying that his people might live, even as Christ died.

Be assured that such a death always means a redemption. Emmet redeemed

Ireland from acquiescence in the Union. His attempt was not a failure, but a triumph for that deathless thing we call Irish Nationality. It was by Emmet that men remembered Ireland until Davis and Mitchel took up his work again, and '48 handed on the tradition to '67 and from '67 we receive the tradition unbroken.

You ask me to speak of the Ireland of today. What need I say but that today Ireland is turning her face once more to the old path? Nothing seems more definitely to emerge when one looks at the movements that are stirring both above the surface and beneath the surface in men's minds at home than the fact that the new generation is reaffirming the Fenian faith, the faith of Emmet. It is because we know that this is so that we can suffer in patience the things that are said and done in the name of Irish Nationality by some of our leaders. What one may call the Westminster phase is passing: the National Movement is swinging back again into its proper channel. A new junction has been made with the past; into the movement that has never wholly died since '67 have come the young men of the Gaelic League. Having renewed communion with its origins, Irish Nationalism is today a more virile thing than ever before in our time. Of that be sure.

I have said again and again that when the Gaelic League was founded in 1893 the Irish Revolution began. The Gaelic League brought it a certain distance upon its way; but the Gaelic League could not accomplish the Revolution. For five or six years a new phase has been due, and lo! It is with us now. Today Ireland is once more organising, once more learning the noble trade of arms. In our towns and country places Volunteer companies are springing up. Dublin pointed the way, Galway has followed Dublin, Cork has followed Galway, Wexford has followed Cork, Limerick has followed Wexford, Monaghan has followed Limerick, Sligo has followed Monaghan, Donegal has followed Sligo. There is again in Ireland the murmur of a marching, and talk of guns and tactics. What this movement may mean for our country no man can say. But it is plain to all that the existence on Irish soil of an Irish army is the most portentous fact that has appeared in Ireland for over a hundred years: a fact which marks definitely the beginning of the second stage of the Revolution which was commenced when the Gaelic League was founded. The inner significance of the movement lies in this, that men of every rank and class, of every section of Nationalist opinion, of every shade of religious belief, have discovered that they share a common patriotism, that their faith is one and that there is one service in which they can come together at last; the service of their country in arms. We are realising now how proud a thing it is to serve, and in the comradeship and joy of the new service we are forgetting many ancient misunderstandings. In the light of a rediscovered citizenship things are plain to us that were before obscure:

"Lo, a clearness of vision has followed, lo, a purification of sight;

Lo, the friend is discerned from the foeman, the wrong recognised from the right."

After all, there are in Ireland but two parties; those who stand for the English connection and those who stand against it. On what side, think you, stand the Irish Volunteers? I cannot speak for the Volunteers; I am not authorised to say when they will use their arms or where or how. I can speak only for myself; and it is strictly a personal perception that I am recording, but a perception that to me is very clear, when I say that before this generation has passed the Volunteers will draw the sword of Ireland. There is no truth but the old truth and no way but the old way. Home Rule may come or may not come, but under Home Rule or in its absence there remains for the Volunteers and for Ireland the substantial business of achieving Irish nationhood. And I do not know how nationhood is achieved except by armed men; I do not know how nationhood is guarded except by armed men.

I ask you, then, to salute with me the Irish Volunteers. I ask you to mark their advent as an augury that, no matter what pledges may be given by men who do not know Ireland – the stubborn soul of Ireland – that nation of ancient faith will never sell her birthright of freedom for a mess of pottage; a mess of dubious pottage, at that. Ireland has been guilty of many meannesses, of many shrinkings back when she should have marched forward; but she will never be guilty of that immense infidelity.

Robert Emmet and the Ireland of today (2)

An Address delivered by Patrick H Pearse at the Emmet Commemoration in the Aeolian Hall, New York, March 9, 1914.

WE WHO SPEAK HERE TONIGHT are the voice of one of the ancient indestructible things of the world. We are the voice of an idea which is older than any empire and will outlast every empire. We and ours, the inheritors of that idea, have been at age-long war with one of the most powerful empires that has ever been built up upon the earth; and that empire will pass before we pass. We are older than England and we are stronger than England. In every generation we have renewed the struggle, and so it shall be unto the end. When England thinks she has trampled out our battle in blood, some brave man rises and rallies us again; when England thinks she has purchased us with a bribe, some good man redeems us by a sacrifice. Wherever England goes on her mission of empire we meet her and we strike at her; yesterday it was on the South African veldt, today it is in the Senate House at Washington, tomorrow it may be in the streets of Dublin. We pursue her like a sleuth-hound; we lie in wait for her and come upon her like a thief in the night; and some day we will overwhelm her with the wrath of God.

It is not that we are apostles of hate. Who like us has carried Christ's word of charity about the earth? But the Christ that said: "My peace I leave you, My peace I give you", is the same Christ that said: "I bring not peace, but a sword". There can be no peace between right and wrong, between truth and falsehood, between justice and oppression, between freedom and tyranny. Between them it is eternal war until the wrong is righted, until the true thing is established, until justice is accomplished, until freedom is won.

So when England talks of peace we know our answer: "Peace with you? Peace while your one hand is at our throat and your other hand is in our pocket? Peace with a footpad? Peace with a pickpocket? Peace with the leech that is sucking our body dry of blood? Peace with the many-armed monster whose tentacles envelop us while its system emits an inky fluid that shrouds its work of murder from the eyes of men? The time has not yet come to talk of peace."

But England, we are told, offers us terms. She holds out to us the hand of friendship. She gives us a Parliament with an Executive responsible to it.

Within two years the Home Rule Senate meets in College Green and King George comes to Dublin to declare its sessions open. In anticipation of that happy event our leaders have proffered England our loyalty. Mr Redmond accepts Home Rule as a "final settlement between the two nations"; Mr O'Brien in the fulness of his heart cries "God Save the King"; Colonel Lynch offers England his sword in case she is attacked by a foreign power.

And so this settlement is to be a final settlement. Would Wolfe Tone have accepted it as a final settlement? Would Robert Emmet have accepted it as a final settlement? Either we are heirs to their principles or we are not. If we are, we can accept no settlement as final which does not *"break the connection England, the never-failing source of all our political evils";* if we are not, how dare we go in annual pilgrimage to Bodenstown, how dare we gather here or anywhere to commemorate the faith and sacrifice of Emmet? Did, then, these dead heroic men live in vain? Has Ireland learned a truer philosophy than the philosophy of '98, and a nobler way of salvation than the way of 1803? Is Wolfe Tone's definition superseded, and do we discharge our duty to Emmet's memory by according him annually our pity?

To do the English justice, I do not think they are satisfied that Ireland will accept Home Rule as a final settlement. I think they are a little anxious today. If their minds were tranquil on the subject of Irish loyalty they would hardly have proclaimed the importation of arms into Ireland the moment the Irish Volunteers had begun to organise themselves. They had given the Ulster faction, which is used as a catspaw by one of the English parties, two years to organise and arm against that Home Rule Bill which they profess themselves so anxious to pass: to the Nationalists of Ireland they did not give two weeks. Of course, we can arm in spite of them: today we are organising and training the men and we have ways and means of getting arms when the men are ready for the arms. The contention I make now, and I ask you to note it well, is that England does not trust Ireland with guns; that under Home Rule or in the absence of Home Rule England declares that we Irish must remain an unarmed people; and England is right.

England is right in suspecting Irish loyalty, and those Irishmen who promise Irish loyalty to England are wrong. I believe them honest; but they have spent so much of their lives parleying with the English, they have sat so often and so long at English feasts, that they have lost communion with the ancient unpurchaseable faith of Ireland, the ancient stubborn thing that forbids, as if with the voice of fate, any loyalty from Ireland to England, any union between us and them, any surrender of one jot or shred of our claim to freedom even in return for all the blessings of the British peace.

I have called that old faith an indestructible thing, I have said that it is more powerful than empires. If you would understand its might you must consider how it has made all the generations of Ireland heroic. Having its root in all gentleness, in a man's love for the place where his mother bore him, for the breast that gave him suck, for the voices of children that sounded in a house now silent, for the faces that glowed around a fireside now cold, for the story told by lips that will not speak again, having its root, I say, in all gentleness, it is yet a terrible thing urging the generations to perilous bloody attempts, nerving men to give up life for the death-in-life of dungeons, teaching little boys to die with laughing lips, giving courage to young girls to bare their backs to the lashes of a soldiery.

It is easy to imagine how the spirit of Irish patriotism called to the gallant and adventurous spirit of Tone or moved the wrathful spirit of Mitchel. In them deep called unto deep: heroic effort claimed the heroic man. But consider how the call was made to a spirit of different, yet not less noble mould; and how it was answered. In Emmet it called to a dreamer and he awoke a man of action; it called to a student and a recluse and he stood forth a leader of men; it called to one who loved the ways of peace and he became a revolutionary. I wish I could help you to realise, I wish I could myself adequately realise, the humanity, the gentle and grave humanity, of Emmet. We are so dominated by the memory of that splendid death of his, by the memory of that young figure, serene and smiling, climbing to the gallows above that sea of silent men in Thomas Street, that we forget the life of which that death was only the necessary completion; and the life has a nearer meaning for us than the death. For Emmet, finely gifted though he was, was just a young man with the same limitations, the same self-questionings, the same falterings, the same kindly human emotions surging up sometimes in such strength as almost to drown a heroic purpose, as many a young man we have known. And his task was just such a task as many of us have undertaken: he had to go through the same repellent routine of work; to deal with the hard, uncongenial details of correspondence and committee meetings; he had the same sordid difficulties that we have, yea, even the vulgar difficulty of want of funds. And he had the same poor human material to work with, men who misunderstood, men who bungled, men who talked too much, men who failed at the last moment . . .

Yes, the task we take up again is just Emmet's task of silent unattractive work, the routine of correspondence and committees and organising. We must face it as bravely and as quietly as he faced it, working on in patience as he worked on, hoping as he hoped; cherishing in our secret hearts the mighty hope that to us, though so unworthy, it may be given to bring to accomplishment the thing he left unaccomplished, but working on even when that hope dies within us.

I would ask you to consider now how the call I have spoken of was made to the spirit of a woman, and how, equally, it was responded to. Wherever Emmet is commemorated let Anne Devlin not be forgotten. Bryan Devlin had a dairy farm in Butterfield Lane; his fields are still green there. Five sons of his fought in '98. Anne was his daughter, and she went to keep house for Emmet when he moved into Butterfield House. You know how she kept vigil there on the night of the rising. When all was lost and Emmet came out in his hurried retreat through Rathfarnham to the mountains, her greeting was – according to tradition it was spoken in Irish, and Emmet must have replied in Irish – "Musha, bad welcome to you! Is Ireland lost by you, cowards that you are, to lead the people to destruction and then to leave them?" "Don't blame me, Anne, the fault is not mine," said Emmet. And she was sorry for the pain her words had inflicted, spoken in the pain of her own disappointment. She would have tended him like a mother could he have tarried there, but his path led to Kilmashogue, and hers was to be a harder duty. When Sirr came out with his soldiery she was still keeping her vigil. "Where is Emmet?" "I have nothing to tell you." To all their questions she had but one answer: "I have nothing to say; I have nothing to tell you." They swung her up to a cart and half-hanged her several times; after each half-hanging she was revived and questioned: still the same answer. They pricked her breast with bayonets until the blood spurted out in their faces. They dragged her to prison and tortured her for days. Not one word did they extract from this steadfast woman. And when Emmet was sold, he was sold, not by a woman, but by a man – by the friend that he had trusted – by the counsel who, having sold him, was to go through the ghastly mockery of defending him at the bar.

The fathers and mothers of Ireland should often tell their children that story of Robert Emmet and that story of Anne Devlin. To the Irish mothers who hear me I would say that when at night you kiss your children and in your hearts call down a benediction, you could wish for your boys no higher thing than that, should the need come, they may be given the strength to make Emmet's sacrifice, and for your girls no greater gift from God than such fidelity as Anne Devlin's.

It is more than a hundred years since these things were suffered; and they were suffered in vain if nothing of the spirit of Emmet and Anne Devlin survives in the young men and young women of Ireland. Does anything of that spirit survive? I think I can speak for my own generation. I think I can speak for my contemporaries in the Gaelic League, an organisation which has not yet concerned itself with politics, but whose younger spirits are accepting the full national idea and are bringing into the national struggle the passion and the practicalness which marked the early stages of the language movement. I think I can speak for the young men of the Volunteers. So far, they have no programme beyond learning the trade of arms: a trade which no man of Ireland could learn for over a hundred years past unless he took the English shilling. It is a good programme; and we may almost commit the future of Ireland to the keeping of the Volunteers. I think I can speak for a younger generation still: for some of the young men that are entering the National University, for my own pupils at St Enda's College, for the boys of Fianna Éireann. To the grey-haired men whom I see on this platform, to John Devoy and Richard Burke, I bring, then, this message from Ireland: that their seed-sowing of forty years ago has not been without its harvest, that there are young men and little boys in Ireland today who remember what they taught and who, with God's blessing, will one day take – or make – an opportunity of putting their teaching into practice.

An Addendum
(August 1914)

Since I spoke the words here reprinted there has been a quick movement of events in Ireland. The young men of the nation stand organised and disciplined, and are rapidly arming themselves; blood has flowed in Dublin Streets, and the cause of the Volunteers has been consecrated by a holocaust. A European war has brought about a crisis which may contain, as yet hidden within it, the moment for which the generations have been waiting. It remains to be seen whether, if that moment reveals itself, we shall have the sight to see and the courage to do, or whether it shall be written of this generation, alone of all the generations of Ireland, that it had none among it who dared to make the ultimate sacrifice.

Arbour Hill

No rising column marks the spot
Where many a victim lies;
But Oh! the blood which here has streamed
To Heaven for justice cries.
It claims it on the oppressor's head
Who joys in human woe,
Who drinks the tears by misery shed
And mocks them as they flow.

It claims it on the callous judge,
Whose hands in blood are dyed,
Who arms injustice with the sword,
The balance throws aside.
It claims it for his ruined isle,
Her wretched children's grave;
Where withered Freedom droops her head,
And man exists – a slave.

O Sacred Justice! Free this land
From tyranny abhorred;
Resume thy balance and thy seat
Resume but sheathe thy sword.
No retribution should we seek
Too long has horror reigned;
By mercy marked may freedom rise,
By cruelty unstained.

Nor shall a tyrant's ashes mix
With those our martyred dead;
This is the place where Erin's sons
In Erin's cause have bled.
And those who here are laid at rest,
Oh! Hallowed be each name;
Their memories are forever blest
Consigned to endless fame.

Unconsecrated is this ground,
Unblest by holy hands;
No bell here tolls its solemn sound,
No monument here stands.
But here the patriots' tears are shed,
The poor man's blessing given;
These consecrate the virtuous dead,
These waft their fame to heaven.

– Robert Emmet (Trebor)

On Robert Emmet's tomb

May the tempests of winter that sweep o'er thy tomb
Disturb not a slumber so sacred as thine;
May the breezes of summer that breathe of perfume
Waft their balmiest dews to so hallowed a shrine.

May the foot of the tyrant, the coward, the slave,
Be palsied with dread where thine ashes repose,
Where that undying shamrock still blooms on thy grave
Which sprung when the dawnlight of Erin arose.

There oft have I marked the grey gravestones among,
Where thy relics distinguished in lowliness lay,
The peasant boy pensively lingering long
And silently weep as he passed away.

And how could he not pause if the blood of his sires
Ever wakened one generous throb in his heart?
How could he inherit a spark of their fires
If tearless and frigid he dared to depart?

Not the scrolls of a court could emblazon thy fame
Like the silence that reigns in the palace of thee,
Like the whispers that pass of thy dearly loved name,
Like the tears of the good, like the groans of the free.

No trump tells thy virtues – the grave where they rest
With thy dust shall remain unpolluted by fame.
Till thy foes, by the world and by fortune caresst
Shall pass like a mist from the light of thy name.

When the storm cloud that lowers o'er the daybeam is gone,
Unchanged, unextinguished its lifespring will shine,
When Erin has ceased with their memory to groan
She will smile thro' the tears of revival on thine.

– Percy Bysshe Shelley

WHEN HE WHO ADORES THEE

In this poem the poet expresses some of the
noble sentiments asserted by Emmet in the dock.

When he who adores thee has left but the name
Of his fault and his sorrow behind,
Oh! say, wilt thou weep when they darken the fame
Of a life that for thee was resigned?
Yes, weep! and, however my foes may condemn,
Thy tears shall efface their decree;
For Heaven can witness, though guilty to them,
I have been but too faithful to thee!

With thee were the dreams of my earliest love
Every thought of my reason was thine;
In my last humble prayer to the Spirit above
Thy name shall be mingled with mine!
Oh! blessed are the lovers and friends who shall live
The days of thy glory to see.
But the next dearest blessing that Heaven can give,
Is the pride of thus dying for thee.

– Thomas Moore

She is far from the Land

She is far from the land where her young hero sleeps
And lovers around her are sighing;
But coldly she turns from their gaze and weeps
For her heart in his grave is lying.

She sings the wild songs of her dear native plains,
Every note which he loved a-waking;
Ah! little they think who delight in her strains,
That the heart of the minstrel is breaking.

He had lived for his love, for his country he died,
They were all that to life had entwined him;
Nor soon shall the tears of his country be dried,
Nor long will his love stay behind him.

Oh! make her a grave where the sunbeams rest,
When they promise a glorious morrow;
They'll shine o'er her sleep, like a smile from the West,
From her own loved island of sorrow.

– Thomas Moore

Oh! Breathe not his Name

Oh! Breathe not his name – let it sleep in the shade
Where cold and unhonoured his relics are laid!
Sad, silent, and dark, be the tears that we shed,
As the night-dew that falls on the grass o'er his head!

Night dew that falls, though in silence it weeps,
Shall brighten with verdure the grave where he sleeps,
And the tear that we shed, though in secret it rolls,
Shall long keep his memory green in our souls.

– Thomas Moore

FORGET NOT THE FIELD

Forget not the field where they perish'd,
The truest, the last of the brave,
All gone – and the bright hopes they cherish'd
Gone with them, and quench'd in their grave.

Oh! Could we from death but recover
Those hearts, as they bounded before,
In the face of high Heaven to fight over
That combat for freedom once more –

Could the chain for an instant be riven
Which Tyranny flung round us then,
Oh! 't is not in Man nor in Heaven,
To let tyranny bind it again!

But it is past – and, though blazon'd in story
The name of our Victor may be,
Accursed is the march of that glory
Which treads o'er the hearts of the free.

Far dearer the grave or the prison
Illumed by one patriot name,
Than the trophies of all who have risen
On liberty's ruins to fame!

– Thomas Moore

THE THREE FLOWERS

One time when walking down a lane,
When night was drawing nigh,
I met a cailín with three flowers,
And she more young than I,
'St Patrick bless you, dear,' said I,
'If you'll be quick and tell
The place where you did find these flowers.
I seem to know so well.'

She took and kissed the first flower once,
And sweetly said to me:
'This flower comes from the Wicklow Hills,
Dew wet and pure,' said she,
'Its name is Michael Dwyer –
The strongest flower of all;
But I'll keep it fresh beside my breast
'Though all the world should fall.'

She took and kissed the next flower twice
And sweetly said to me:
'This flower I culled on Antrim hill,
Outside Belfast,' said she.
'The name I call it is Wolfe Tone –
The bravest flower of all;
But I'll keep it fresh beside my breast
'Though all the world should fall.'

She took and kissed the next flower thrice,
And softly said to me:
'This flower I found in Thomas Street,
In Dublin fair,' said she.
'It's name is Robert Emmet,
The youngest flower of all;
But I'll keep it fresh beside my breast,
'Though all the world should fall.'

'Then Emmet, Dwyer and Tone I'll keep,
For I do love them all;
And I'll keep them fresh beside my breast
'Though all the world should fall.'   **– Norman G Reddin**

Bold Robert Emmet

The struggle is over, the boys are defeated,
Old Ireland's surrounded by sadness and gloom,
We were defeated and shamefully treated,
And I, Robert Emmet, awaiting my doom.
Hung, drawn and quartered, sure that was my sentence,
But soon I will show them no coward am I,
My crime is the love of the land I was born in,
A hero I lived and a hero I'll die.

Chorus:
Bold Robert Emmet, the darling of Erin,
Bold Robert Emmet will die with a smile,
Farewell companions both loyal and daring,
I'll lay down my life for the Emerald Isle.

The barque lay at anchor awaiting to bring me
Over the billows to the land of the free;
But I must see my sweetheart for I know she will cheer me,
And with her I will sail far over the sea.
But I was arrested and cast into prison,
Tried as a traitor, a rebel, a spy;
But no man can call me a knave or a coward,
A hero I lived and a hero I'll die.

Chorus:

Hark! the bell's tolling, I know well its meaning,
My poor heart tells me it is my death knell;
In come the clergy, the warder is leading,
I have no friends here to bid me farewell.
Goodbye, old Ireland, my parents and sweetheart,
Companions in arms to forget you must try;
I am proud of the honour, it was only my duty –
A hero I lived and a hero I'll die.

Chorus:

Young Emmet

In Green St. court-house in eight-een and three stood young Em-met the he-ro true and brave, for fight-ing the ty-rant his coun-try to free and to tear from her brow the bond of slav-er-y. There are still men in Ire-land both loy-al and true, who rem em-ber her pat-ri-ots with pride, And with God's help young Em-met will soon give to you the epi-taph un-writ-ten since you died.

In Green Street courthouse in eighteen and three
Stood Young Emmet the hero true and brave.
For fighting the tyrant, his country to free
And to tear from her brow the bond of slavery.

Chorus:
There are still men in Ireland, both loyal and true
Who remember her patriots with pride.
And with God's help, young Emmet, we'll soon give to you
The epitaph unwritten since you died.

Alone and defiant, he stood in the dock
While Lord Norbury, the hanging judge, looked down.
Against his false charges, stood firm as a rock,
Another Irish martyr for the Crown.

Chorus:

The verdict was guilty, the sentence was death
And in Thomas Street the tyrant's work was done.
But Young Emmet smiled as he drew his last breath,
For he knew the fight for freedom would be won.

Chorus (2):   **– Paidí Bán Ó Broin**

By Memory Inspired

Air: An Crúiscín Lán

By memory inspired, and love of country fired
The deeds of men I love to dwell upon;
And the patriotic glow of my spirit must bestow
A tribute to the heroes that are gone, boys, gone –
Here's a health to John Mitchel that is gone!

In October, 'Ninety-Seven – may his soul find rest in heaven –
William Orr to execution was led on;
The jury, drunk, agreed that Irish was his creed,
For perjury and threats drove them on, boys on –
Here's the memory of the friends that are gone!

In 'Ninety-Eight – the month, July – the informer's pay was high
When Reynolds gave the gallows brave McCann:
But McCann was Reynolds' first – one could not allay his thirst –
So he brought up Bond and Byrne that are gone, boys, gone –
Here's the memory of the friends that are gone.

We saw a nation's tears shed for John and Henry Sheares.
Betrayed by Judas, Captain Armstrong;
We may forgive, but yet we never can forget
The fate of Tone and Emmet that are gone, boys, gone.
Of all the fearless heroes that are gone.

How did Lord Edward die? Like a man, without a sigh,
But he left his handiwork on Major Swan!
But Sirr, with steel-clad breast, and coward heart at best,
Left us cause to mourn Lord Edward that is gone, boys, gone –
Here's the memory of our friends that are gone!

September, Eighteen-three, closed this cruel history,
When Emmet's blood the scaffold flowed upon.
Oh, had our men been wise they then might realise
Their freedom – but we drink to Mitchel that is gone, boys, gone –
Here's the memory of the heroes that are gone!

My Emmet's no more

Air: 'S a Mhuirnín Dílis

Despair in her wild eye, a daughter of Erin
Appeared on the cliff of a bleak rocky shore,
Loose in the winds flowed her dark streaming ringlets
And heedless she gazed on the dread surge's roar.
Loud rang her harp in wild tones of despairing,
The time past away with the present comparing,
And in soul-thrilling strains deeper sorrow declaring,
She rang Erin's woes and her Emmet's no more.

Oh, Erin, my country! your glory's departed,
For tyrants and traitors have stabbed thy heart's core,
Thy daughters have laid in the streams of affliction,
Thy patriots have fled or lie stretched in their gore!
Ruthless ruffians now prowl through thy hamlets forsaken –
From pale hungry orphans their last morsel have taken –
The screams of thy females no pity awaken,
Alas! my poor country, your Emmet's no more!

Brave was his spirit, yet mild as the Brahmin,
His heart bled in anguish at the wrongs of the poor;
To relieve their hard suffering he braved every danger,
The vengeance of tyrants undauntedly bore.
Even before him the proud villains in power
Were seen, though in ermine, in terror to cower,
But alas! he is gone, he has fallen a young flower,
They have murdered my Emmet – my Emmet's no more.

Emmet's Farewell to his Love

Farewell love, farewell love, I'm now going to leave you,
The pale moon is shining her last beams on me,
In truth I do swear that I never deceived thee,
For next to my heart was green Erin and thee.

Come near to my bosom my first and fond true love,
And cherish the heart which beats only for thee,
And let my cold grave with laurels be strewed love,
For I die for my country, green Erin, and thee.

Oh, never again in the moonlight we will roam, love,
When birds are at rest and the stars they do shine,
Oh, never again will I kiss thy sweet lips, love,
Or wander by streamlet with thy hands pressed in mine.

But should another love make you forget me,
Oh, give me a promise before that I die,
That you'll come to my grave when all others forget me,
And there with the soft winds breathe sigh for sigh.

My hour is approaching, let me take one fond look, love,
And watch thy pure beauty till my soul does depart;
Let thy ringlets fall on my face and my brow, love,
Draw near till I press thee to my fond and true heart.

Farewell love, farewell love, the words are now spoken,
The pale moon is shining her last beams on me,
Farewell love, farewell love, I hear the death token,
Never more in this wide world young Emmet you'll see.

On the Uninscribed Tomb of Robert Emmet

"Pray tell me," I said, to an old man who stayed,
Drooping over the grave, which his own hands had made,
"Pray, tell me the name of the tenant who sleeps,
'Neath yonder cold shade, where the sad willow weeps.
Every stone is engraved with the name of the dead,
But yon black slab declares not whose spirit is fled."

In silence he bowed and then beckoned me nigh,
Till we stood o'er the grave – then he said with a sigh,
"Yes, they dare not to trace e'en a word on this stone,
To the memory of him who lies coldly and lone:
He told, them, commanded, the lines o'er his grave
Should never be traced by the hand of a slave."

"He bade them to shade e'en his name in the gloom,
Till the morning of freedom should shine on his tomb,
'When the flag of my country at liberty flies,
Then, then let my name and my monument rise,'
You see they obeyed him – 'tis thirty-two years,
And they still come to moisten his grave with their tears."

"He was young like yourself, and aspired to o'erthrow,
The tyrants, who filled his loved Island with woe.
They crushed him – this earth was too base, too confined;
Too gross for the range of his luminous mind."
The old man then paused, and went slowly away,
And I felt, as he left me, an impulse to pray.

"Great Heaven! I may see, ere my days are done.
A monument rise o'er my country's lost son,
And, oh proudest task be it thus to indite,
The long delayed tribute a freeman must write.
Till then shall its theme in my heart deeply dwell
So peace to thy slumbers – dear Emmet farewell."

– Thomas Kennedy

*This song was obviously written in 1835. See live five of the third stanza.
It is to be found in the English translation of the
Comtesse d'Haussonville's biography of Emmet, published in 1858.*

EMMET

"Ná greantar leac dom is ná cantar m'fheartlaoi
Go mbeidh saoirse cheart ag mo mhíle grá;
Ag an tír tá céasta 's go mór i ngéibheann
Ag Gallaibh bréagach' is ag Gaelaibh tláth'."

Sin a' chaint dhein Emmet ar lá a dhaortha,
Agus fós tá Gaela fé smacht na nGall;
Gan splanc 'na gcroíthe de spiorad na saoirse-
Táid casta, claoite ag an smíst' úd thall.

Comrádaithe Emmet, idir óg agus críonna,
Táid fós ag líonadh na gcarcar ngránn';
Táid fós dá lámhach, ag tál na méirleach;
Táid fós dá gcéasadh ar an scálán ard!

Ach lasfar lóchrann do Phoblacht Éireann,
Agus scaipfear néalta na mbrad 's na mbréag;
Beidh a ghuí ag Emmet agus críoch lena shaothar,
Agus saoirse ag Gaelaibh arís go héag!

– Brian na Banban

A Biography in French

ONE OF THE EARLIEST biographies of Robert Emmet was written by a French woman, Louise de Broglie, Comtesse d'Haussonville, an outspokenly independent and liberal woman, and published in Paris in 1858. She was a grand-daughter of the famous Madame de Staël.

The book was translated from the French by John P Leonard and published in Belfast in the same year. We can read in the diary of the Co Down Young Irelander, "Honest" John Martin, that he was in Paris that year and that the translation and publication were organised by himself, the Comtesse and Miles Byrne. It is interesting to note the imprint on this English edition. It reads:

> "Printed and published by D. Holland at the 'Ulsterman' office."

Between the title page and the beginning of the text, there is an extra page on which we can read:

> "I undertook the publication (of this book) because no one else would. In England, publishers refused the work, lest this French eulogy of a young Irish martyr-patriot should injure the 'cordial alliance'. In Dublin, those whose trade is printing and publishing feared the risk, with the petty trader's timidity—some, too, would not offend the Castle.
>
> In this emergency, I (though neither printer nor publisher) undertook the risk, that so good a book might not be lost to the Irish public."
>
> D. Holland."

The translator was so impressed with the author's French translation of Emmet's speech from the dock that he included a lengthy footnote in which he gave her French version of the peroration. As a translator, he appreciated the skill she displayed in rendering the speech in an appropriate style and form. For those who may be interested, this is the text:

"My lords, vous attendez avec impatience votre victime. Tout l'artifice de terreurs dont vous l'avez entourée, n'a pas glacé dans ses veines le sang dont vous êtes avides, et tout à l'heure, il criera vengeance au ciel; mais patience encore. Je n'ai plus que peu de mots à dire; je marche à mon froid et muet tombeau. Le flambeau de ma vie est presque éteint. Je me suis séparé, pour la cause de mon pays, de tout ce qui m'était cher dans la vie, de l'idole de mon âme, de l'objet de mon affection. Il ne me reste plus qu'à recevoir ma récompense. Ma course est terminée. La tombe s'ouvre pour me recevoir, et je vais disparaître dans son sein.

"Je n'ai qu'une demande à faire au monde en le quittant: c'est la charité de son silence. Qu'aucun homme n'écrive mon épitaphe, car aucun homme connaissant mes motifs n'oserait aujourd'hui les défendre; qu'on ne souffre pas que l'ignorance et le préjugé les accusent. Qu'ils reposent dans l'obscurité et la paix; que ma mémoire soit laissée dans l'oubli; que ma tombe reste sans inscription jusqu'à ce que d'autres temps et d'autres hommes puissent rendre justice à mon caractère. Quand mon pays aura repris son rang parmi les nations de la terre, alors, mais seulement alors, que mon épitaphe soit écrite. J'ai fini."

Is álainn an friotal é. Ach ní bheadh sé ceart focail scoir Emmet a thabhairt i bhFraincis gan iad a thabhairt i nGaeilge freisin. Seo, mar sin, leagan Gaeilge, aistrithe go galánta ag Dáithí Ó hÓgáin, ar bhealach atá ag cur leis an ábhar:

"A thiarnaí, tá cíocras na híobartha ag cur oraibh. An fhuil seo atá uaibh, ní téachtaithe di ó na bréag-uafáis atá timpeall ar an íobartach. Ina sruth te bríomhar di trí na cuisleanna a chruthaigh Dia di le haidhmeanna uaisle, cuisleanna atá fúibhse a scrios anois le haidhmeanna chomh gránna is go bhfuil a n-uaill ag éirí chun na bhflaitheas. Ach bíodh foighne go fóill agaibh! Níl ach beagán focal eile le rá agam. Tá m'aghaidh ar an uaigh, gona fuaire is a tost ar fad. Is gairid eile do lóchrann na beatha ionam go múchfar í. Seo scartha agam le gach ar ghean liom den saol seo ar son mo thíre; agus mo chúl tugtha le seoid eile dá dtug mé adhradh ó chroí, í siúd ar a bhfuil mo shearc. Tá mo rás rite. Tá béal na huaighe ar leathadh romham agus mé ag teannadh lena hucht.

"Níl ach an t-aon achainí amháin agam agus mé ag fágáil an tsaoil seo. Is é sin, mar charthanacht, an tost. Ná bíodh aon duine ag scríobh feartlaoi dom; mar aon duine ar eol dó mo mhianta ní leomhfadh anois iad a chur i gcrích, agus dá réir sin ná ligtear don chlaontacht ná don aineolas smál a chur orthu. Fágtar faoi chlúid is faoi shuaimhneas iad, agus fágtar mo thuama gan scríbhinn agus mo chuimhne ar dearmad nó go dtiocfaidh ré eile agus dream eile a sheasóidh ceart dom. Nuair a bheidh a hionad á ghlacadh ag mo thírse i measc náisiúin na cruinne, is ansin agus ansin amháin, a bheidh m'fheartlaoi le scríobh. Sin deireadh agam."

BIBLIOGRAPHY

Broglie, Louise de, Comtesse d'Haussonville: *Robert Emmet.*

Byrne, Miles: *Memoirs of Miles Byrne.*

Dickson, Charles MD: *The Life of Michael Dwyer.*

Elliott, Marianne: *Partners in Revolution, The United Irishmen and France.*

Emmet, TA: *Memoir of Thomas Addis and Robert Emmet.*

Geoghegan, Patrick M: *Robert Emmet, A Life.*

Landreth, Helen: *The Pursuit of Robert Emmet.*

McDowell, RB and Webb, DA: *Trinity College Dublin, 1592-1952 An Academic History.*

Mac Giolla Easpaig, SN: *Tomás Ruiséil.*

Madden, Richard R: *The United Irishmen, Their Lives and Times.*

Madden, Richard R: *The Life and Times of Robert Emmet Esq.*

Mitchel, John: *The History of Ireland.*

Ó Broin, Leon: *Emmet.*

Ó Broin, Leon: *The Unfortunate Mr Robert Emmet.*

O'Hegarty, PS: *A History of Ireland under the Union.*

Ó hUiginn., Brian: *Inis Teoin, Wolfe Tone Annual, 1941 and 1953.*

Postgate, Raymond W: *Robert Emmet.*

Reynolds, JJ: *Footprints of Emmet.*